insight text guide

Deborah Rechter

The Wife of Martin Guerre

Janet Lewis

First published in 2003, reprinted in 2004, 2011. Reprinted with amendments in 2016, 2017, 2020.

Insight Publications Pty Ltd
3/350 Charman Road
Cheltenham VIC 3192
Australia
Tel: +61 3 8571 4950
Fax: +61 3 8571 0257
Email: books@insightpublications.com.au

www.insightpublications.com.au

National Library of Australia Cataloguing-in-Publication entry:
Rechter, Deborah
Insight text guide: The Wife of Martin Guerre, Janet Lewis
For secondary and tertiary students.
ISBN 9781920693169
1. Lewis, Janet, 1899-. Wife of Martin Guerre. I. Title.
(Series : Insight text guide).
813.52

Other ISBNs:
9781922525048 (digital)
9781922525031 (bundle: print + digital)

Cover design: Gisela Beer, based on a concept by The Modern Art Production Group

Printed in Australia by Ligare

contents

CHARACTER MAP

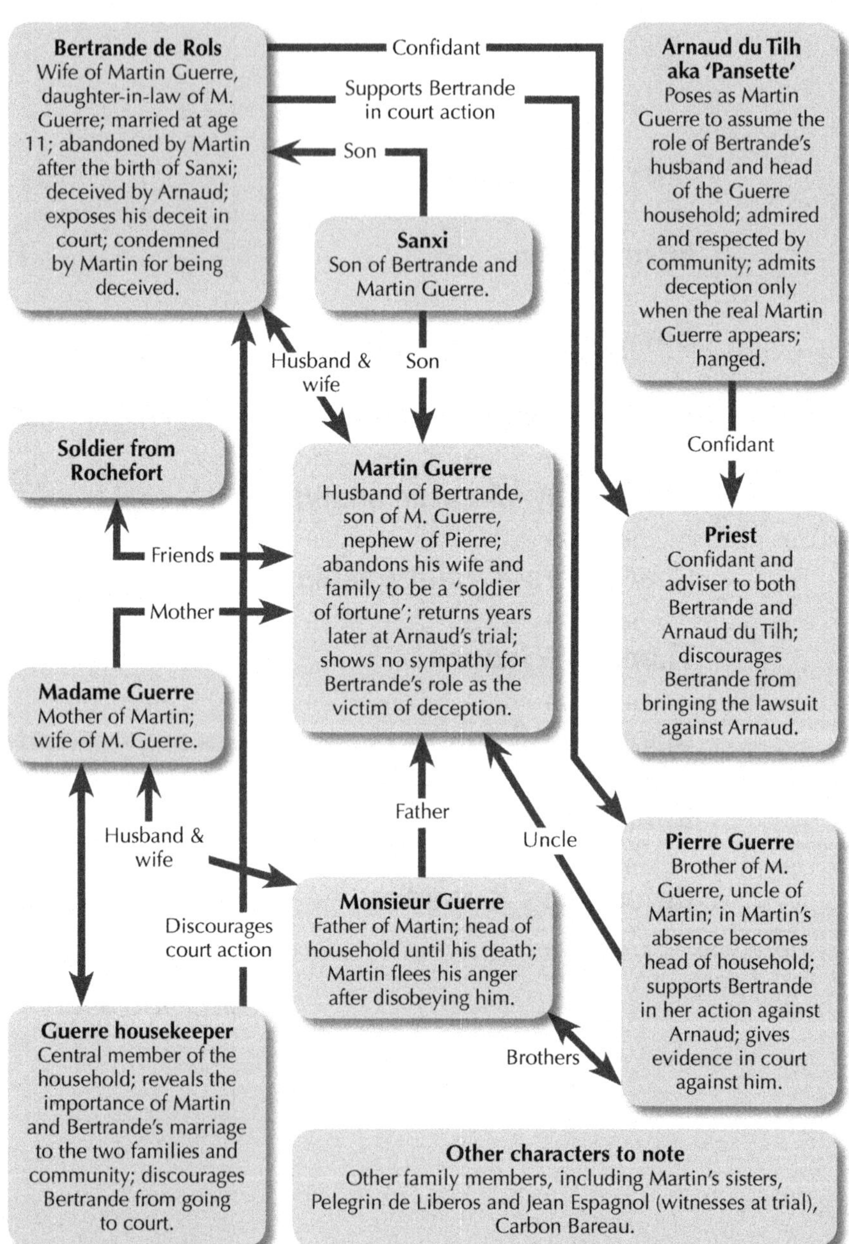

INTRODUCTION

Janet Lewis was born in 1899 in the United States of America. She was an academic and writer who taught creative writing at Stanford University and then English Literature at the University of California, Berkeley. Lewis married well-known American critic and poet Yvor Winters, and together they became the centre of an exclusive literary circle.

As a young woman, Janet Lewis had tuberculosis and lived in the shadow of death for five years. History had always interested her, and she explored the past in her books. Lewis said that she was fascinated by kitchens and they often featured in her fiction. She is said to have had a great sense of humour.

Lewis spent some time in France, both as a young graduate and again in 1951 while on a Guggenheim Fellowship. She became interested in legal fiction when her husband gave her a book containing a collection of famous legal cases based on circumstantial evidence, hoping to give her a source of inspiration for her fiction. The novella, *The Wife of Martin Guerre*, and two of her other books were based on cases she discovered in that collection. *The Wife of Martin Guerre* was perhaps her most famous publication, although she regarded herself as primarily a poet.

She died in 1998, having lived almost one hundred years.

The Wife of Martin Guerre

The Wife of Martin Guerre is a novella based on the real sixteenth-century trial of Arnaud du Tilh, who was tried for impersonating another. It invents the background and context for the trial, including the lifestyle and family life of the accuser, Bertrande de Rols. As the title of the novella suggests, Bertrande's story is the focus of the narrative.

In 1983 Natalie Zemon Davis published a history book exploring the trial. Her book is called *The Return of Martin Guerre*. This is not a work of fiction like Lewis's. Rather, it is a detailed and complex analysis of the events referred to in the novella. It has a very different perspective on, and interpretation of, the events, based on systematic historical research. As Zemon Davis wrote, 'The charming novel by Janet Lewis, *The Wife of Martin Guerre*, differs from my historical account in most respects, but they resemble each other in presenting a Bertrande who is not a dupe and who has some independence of spirit.' Indeed, Zemon Davis argues that Bertrande realised early on that the man who returned to her was an impostor and willingly became involved in Arnaud du Tilh's deception. *The Return of Martin Guerre* is worth reading for the insight and background it provides for understanding *The Wife of Martin Guerre*; however, it is important to remember that the story under consideration here is the one by Janet Lewis, so be careful not to confuse the two.

Zemon Davis was also the historical advisor for the film of the same name based on her book. The film is informative, especially in relation to the historical context in which the text is set.

BACKGROUND & CONTEXT

Setting

The novella is set in rural southern France in the sixteenth century. Many important aspects of society in that time and place were quite different from today, including the physical landscape, the social hierarchy, the meaning of family, the role of religion and the monarchy. As historian Norman Davies puts it in *Europe: A History* (1996):

> Imagining the Middle Ages is, indeed, the problem. Historians have to stress not just what the medieval scene contained but also what it lacked. In its physical surroundings, it lacked many of the sights, sounds and smells that have since become commonplace. There were no factory chimneys, no background traffic noise, no artificial pollutants or deodorants.

Social context

Bertrande's spiritual background

Medieval Europe was preoccupied with religion. Historians describe this era as 'theocratic', that is, having a system of government in which the church had great power and influence. Religion was of great importance in the daily lives of individuals. Everything was attributable to God. All areas of life – daily activities, areas of learning such as philosophy, art, science, as well as what was thought of as right and wrong – were constructed around a notion of God, and done in the service of God.

In Bertrande's village of Artigues, religion affects everyday life and every villager's actions. Bertrande herself is a pious woman. She knows and believes in the teachings of the Catholic church and lives her life accordingly. Her devotion and understanding of sin is critical to the story.

Bertrande's morality and actions are guided by the rules and conventions of her religion.

The priest in a small village, such as Artigues, would conduct religious ceremonies in the local church, regularly visit surrounding farms and act as a spiritual advisor and counsellor. As one of the few literate men in the area – that is, one of the few who could read and write – he would deal with any business and legal matters on behalf of the peasant farmers. We see this in Lewis's portrait of the parish priest.

Rural life

Medieval people had a different sense of space from that which we experience today. In France in the sixteenth century only one in twenty lived in a city of at least 10,000, and 90 percent lived in villages of only a few hundred. Transport was limited and unreliable. Travel was by horse or on foot and therefore slow, and rural communities were isolated. This meant that communities such as Artigues had little regular contact with larger towns and cities. The persistence of the feudal system, the importance of religion and the focus on communal living can all be understood in the context of this isolation. In the villages in southern France, houses were grouped and well-organised. Villages held market days for the exchange of produce, and there was considerable traffic between local towns. However, even amongst the most prosperous peasants a second set of clothes was a luxury. Villagers were mostly illiterate. Apart from the priest there may have been a notary (lawyer or secretary) in the village to perform necessary tasks, such as preparing property or agricultural contracts. According to historian Natalie Zemon Davis, Artigues had a kind of council consisting of three or four local elders approved by the judge at Rieux who heard minor disputes. (Note that 'Artiguat' is apparently the correct spelling of the name of the historical village in which these events took place. Lewis uses the spelling 'Artigues' perhaps because she used a second-hand account for her research – see 'Afterword'. This also emphasises the fact that her novel is fiction.)

Farming life

Time in a farming community is cyclical. The rhythm of life is dependent upon the seasons and the weather. Spring and summer are spent preparing for the winter. Bertrande and Martin are married in winter when the cold weather means little farm work is possible and the roads to other villages are impassable because of the snow. 'It was a season of leisure in which weddings might well be celebrated' (p.5).

The farm buildings would have been laid out in a square: a paved courtyard before the main house, with the dairy, barn and storerooms on either side. Bertrande's mother-in-law shows the young bride the buildings in which domestic and farm activities take place, and where and how the farm's produce is preserved and stored. She also tells her new daughter-in-law how the work tasks are allocated (p.15). On her first night in the household Bertrande is waited upon at dinner, but after that she must serve the assembled farm labourers and male family members.

According to the historical research, villagers in Artigues were either small independent land owners and farmers, farm labourers, or craftsmen and skilled workers. Wheat, millet, oats, grapes, cows, goats and sheep were cultivated in and around the village. Agriculture was carried out for personal and extended familial gain, but individual and communal interests meshed tightly. Family and community support were essential to personal security and survival in an unpredictable world. People were dependent on good weather for food and on other people's good will when the dangers of wildlife, thieves, or hunger as a result of bad crops threatened survival. The marriage of Martin and Bertrande is an example of how community and family advantage was considered more important than individual desires.

Women

Medieval notions of women's physiology provide clues about social understandings of women. There was not much science and a lot of superstition that surrounded the medieval medical model. Women were considered to be physically and mentally hampered by having a uterus.

The so-called disease 'hysteria' included every discomfort experienced by women and was thought to be caused by the movement of the womb around the body. Within this belief system, which linked a person's physical and psychological characteristics, women were also considered changeable, deceptive and tricky.

Women were understood to be highly sexual beings with insatiable sexual appetites. That men felt vulnerable to the lusts of women, and jealously guarded their rights to sexual possession of their women, helps to explain the legal and religious intolerance for sexual relations outside marriage. Certainly, the threat of God's punishment for adultery works effectively on Bertrande.

Married women had no independent existence under the law. They could neither own nor sell property. Once married, the husband assumed possession of the property the wife brought to the marriage. In the text of the wedding ceremony and in understandings about marriage, man and wife became one identity and the man was their representative in the public sphere. It was assumed that a household could have only one head. A married woman could not testify in court, for example, because it was assumed that her husband would speak for her and that they would have a single perspective.

Despite this, rural women had significant farming responsibilities looking after fruit and vegetable growing, poultry and other barnyard animals, and dairy production. They sold produce at markets to supplement the family's income. They were also involved in hard manual labour during harvesting, when the crops were cut by hand with scythes and tied into sheaves. Widows often took on the running of their husband's trade or business after his death.

Family life

In sixteenth-century France, the term 'family' included all those related by blood or marriage, as well as their dependants, not just the nuclear family of one or two parents and their children, which tends to be the meaning today. Often, as we see in *The Wife of Martin Guerre*, several generations lived together under one roof. The household also included the servants and farm workers. When Bertrande marries Martin she becomes incorporated into the household of her husband's family. Young couples did not have a separate bedroom or other private space in which to be by themselves. The ideas of privacy and personal space were not articulated or valued at that time.

This kind of family organisation can be understood in the context of everyday life. In a rural setting in which the first priority was to feed, clothe and house people, each family member was responsible for some part of daily life and for the general security of the household. Family life was also affected by the shorter life expectancy – knowledge of disease prevention and medicine was limited, half of all children died before the age of ten, and death in conflict was a real possibility at a time of fierce religious and territorial disputes. In the event of a death, other family members had to take on the work and responsibilities of the dead person. This was critical for the family's survival. The emphasis was on looking after the group and serving the community, not on the satisfaction of individual needs and desires, as is often the case today.

Marriage

There were four institutions that regulated marriage in southern France in the sixteenth century.

- Arranged marriages were common for members of the social class to which Bertrande and Martin belonged, as their marriage demonstrates. Where property transfer was of issue, parental consent was required and details of the transaction were contained in the marriage contract. Where property was not a concern parental consent was less important.
- Before 1789 marriage was regarded as a matter between the couple rather than a concern for the church or state. Nonetheless, the Catholic church did have some involvement because marriage was one of the 'sacraments' (an act made holy by the church). The church tried to exercise power over people by regulating marriage.

It tried to rule against the marriage of people related by blood – brothers, sisters and cousins, for example. It also regulated sexual relations, insisted that Catholics marry Catholics, and insisted on the free will of the couple.

- The state chose to intervene in royal and noble marriages where power and property were considerations. In 1556, a law was passed that allowed parents to disinherit children who wed without their consent. In 1579, King Henry III ordered greater publicity of impending marriages and threatened the death penalty for anyone who eloped with a minor.
- The community could also attach stigma to unions perfectly reasonable to the civil and religious authorities, so couples marrying without parental consent risked distancing themselves from the wider community also.

Primogeniture

'Primogeniture' is the name given to a legal system of inheritance that favours the eldest male. It was the traditional model of inheritance in England and also operated in France in the sixteenth century to some degree. It is significant in the world of the text, in which Martin, an only son, stands to inherit the estate and all responsibilities for it – to the exclusion of his sisters – on his father's death. It is clear that Martin and Bertrande are married so that the estates of the Guerre and de Rols families become united. Bertrande seems not to be involved with the property of her family of origin. In accordance with the usual practice, Bertrande would have brought a substantial dowry of land to be incorporated into that of her husband's family holdings.

Political context

Religious reform in southern France

By the early sixteenth century, Protestantism had begun to flourish across Europe. Protestantism, led by the German monk Martin Luther

(1483–1546), emerged out of the rejection of Catholic religious practices and ideas. This challenge to the power of the Catholic church caused ongoing religious and political tension in the region and led to frequent and bloody conflict. Religious beliefs often implied political allegiances as well, indeed, religion and political power were often part of the same mix.

There is insufficient space here for a detailed discussion of the differences between Catholicism and Protestantism. However, it is worth following this up in greater detail because reference is made to religious conflict in the text, and the rise of Protestantism had a significant influence on the history of the period. When Martin returns, the reader learns that he has been fighting in just such a battle. The massacre at Amboise, in which Catholics were murdered by Protestants, is the topic of conversation at the inn where Bertrande stays on her journey to the trial at Toulouse (p.79). In this environment, a difference of religious opinion is a matter of great consequence, even of life and death. The degree of intolerance and bitterness is demonstrated by the execution of Maître Jean de Coras, recording judge of Arnaud du Tilh's case, who was found hanging 'from an elm tree in the courtyard of the Château Narbonnais' in 1572 (p.95).

Briefly, Protestantism is based upon followers having a direct relationship with God, rather than through the clergy, as with Catholicism. A central issue between the old and new religions concerns the notion of 'transubstantiation': the Catholic belief that the Eucharist (the bread and wine that are together one of the sacraments central to Christian worship) is actually transformed into the body of Christ during the Mass. Protestants believe that the Eucharist serves a symbolic function only. There are also differences in the forms of worship that reflect their approaches. Protestants traditionally have a simpler personal and religious style.

The rise of Protestantism in the sixteenth century is generally regarded by historians as due to its appeal particularly to urban, educated or entrepreneurial people. It also appealed especially to women. Catholicism is regarded as a more conservative religion that found followers in the country, among the peasants and the aristocracy.

Feudal system

The text is more specific about the feudal system to which Martin is subject. The feudal system was a form of rule that regulated personal and political relationships based on conditions of mutual service and dependence. Norman Davies (1996) writes of feudalism that it 'consisted of a dense network of contractual relationships which linked the highest to the lowest in the realm'. In a statement with particular relevance to Martin's position, Davies says, 'almost everyone was conditioned by their position in the social order. Hemmed in by their legal and emotional ties of dependence. Those ties gave them a measure of security and an unquestioned framework of identity; but they also made individuals vulnerable to exploitation, repression, and involuntary ignorance'.

According to this system and in ways described in the text, Martin owes allegiance to his father and has the legal status of minor until his father's death. At that time Martin will assume possession and responsibility for the entire estate. The text makes it clear that this system reinforces both the absolute power of the patriarch and the security of the farm (p.17). It is also clear that, as the wife of the heir, Bertrande is responsible for household management and the welfare of the children and servants, and even has authority over her sisters-in-law.

Legal system

In the sixteenth century, those under the rule of the French king were not unified under one legal system. In nearly every province there was a separate written legal code and set of legal procedures that the Crown had long sought to centralise without much success. Southern French law was primarily based on canon (religious) law and strongly influenced by Roman law that had been introduced to the region one thousand years before.

The court of Toulouse, which heard the second trial of Arnaud du Tilh, was established only in 1443. It was the first of such institutions outside Paris and it was established as part of an attempt to standardise regional law codes and reinforce allegiance to the king. Clerks of the court held significant power and their positions were often purchased. Many legal positions were hereditary, passed from father to son.

GENRE, STYLE & STRUCTURE

Genre

Historical fiction

The Wife of Martin Guerre is a novella, that is, a short novel. Because it is set in the distant past, it belongs to the category of historical fiction. Historical novels take their setting and often their characters from history, and require research for the preparation of the narrative. The trial of Arnaud du Tilh was a notorious case that received much attention at the time, and has been of interest in the centuries since. The book's 'Afterword' reveals that Lewis loosely based her novella on a report of the appeal by one of the judges present, Jean de Coras. This kind of firsthand documentation is referred to as a primary source. It comes directly from the historical event that is of interest. Lewis did not have access to the original report, however, but worked from a nineteenth-century rough translation of the primary source (p.95).

Q How accurately can Lewis's novella represent history?

Q How necessary is it that historical fiction be historically accurate?

Q What is the point of writing a fictional account of an historical event?

Bildungsroman

The Wife of Martin Guerre might also be considered to belong to a genre of literature called the *Bildungsroman* – a genre first developed by German novelists based on the literal meaning of the word – 'formation novel'. The genre consists of novels which are an

> ... account of the youthful development of a hero or heroine (usually the former). It describes the process by which maturity is achieved through the various ups and downs of life. (Cuddon 1992)

One characteristic of the genre is that it pays greater attention to the 'downs' than 'ups', focusing on the individual's struggles rather than on their successes in life. However, while the hero of a *Bildungsroman* is often a sensitive young man who turns to the arts for creative expression and to relieve the alienation he feels, Bertrande has no such outlet. Her difficulties are real and she turns to the law for help. Instead of relief she is further alienated by the legal system and its processes.

Style

Narrative voice

The narrative voice of *The Wife of Martin Guerre* is best described as 'third-person limited'. The narrator is external to the action. Bertrande is referred to in the third person, as in the example, 'Bertrande had not spoken to Martin in all her life until that morning' (pp.5–6). The narrative is *limited* however, because the story is told from the perspective of Bertrande, although not in her voice. The example above demonstrates this also.

Only limited information is given about other characters in *The Wife of Martin Guerre*. This is particularly clear and meaningful with respect to Martin Guerre. When he appears as a character in the beginning of the book, some of his internal motivation is given (p.7). This is information that comes from an omniscient narrator and contributes to the development of Martin's character and the plot, but would not be available to Bertrande, who is ostensibly the subject of the narrative. This third-person omniscient narrative perspective, in which the narrator can access any character's consciousness, describing their feelings and perceptions as they experience them, is used occasionally in the novella. It allows for the thoughts of some of the characters to be presented where these are important. For example, the reader is given access to Sanxi's thoughts and feelings on the return of his 'father' (pp.38–41), which reinforces the value to the family of the 'impostor'.

From the time of Martin's disappearance, however, there is no further access to his thoughts or feelings, and no reference to his activities. This emphasises the effect of his disappearance on his wife, the subject of the story. Similarly we have no information about the thoughts or independent actions of the impostor, Arnaud du Tilh.

Key point

The limited narration focuses attention on the experience of Bertrande. It allows the reader to become involved in the mystery at the heart of the novella, as Martin Guerre is only revealed to the reader when he appears in the courtroom at Toulouse in the denouement (final scene) of the text.

By considering the internal life of the characters, the narrative allows for the development of certain themes and issues. Bertrande's isolation and loneliness, for example, are made evident through descriptions of both her physical and internal worlds.

> Bertrande, who had continued to stand with her back to the room, her eyes upon the hearth, turned now and looked about her. She was entirely alone. In the courtyard the servants shouted their last farewells. She heard Sanxi's voice.
>
> "Good-bye, my father, my dear father!" (p.62)

The narrative is written in the past tense. The language is formal and somewhat old-fashioned, appropriate to the time in which the text is set. Both narrative and dialogue are written in this language. There is also some use of French that is consistent with the text's setting.

The frequent use of dialogue brings immediacy to the telling of the story. There is more frequent use of dialogue in the trial scenes, and the language in these sections has a very formal and rather stilted style that is appropriate to the courtroom setting.

Narrative style and imagery

The narrative style is realist; places and things are generally described in a realistic fashion. For instance, there are very detailed descriptions of domestic and farm life that evoke the lifestyle and culture of the time. Bertrande's mother-in-law guides her around the farm and house on her first day in the household (pp.14–15). This serves the duel purpose of describing the scene of a sixteenth-century country estate, while driving the narrative forward.

Landscape

The landscape is depicted in detail and is used to mirror the emotional life of the heroine. The most obvious example occurs on the journey to Toulouse for the appeal. As they leave Artigues the environment is lush and fertile. As they journey closer to their destination the landscape becomes harsh and dry. The insects are menacing and the sun unbearable for riding. As they ride through this increasingly desolate country Bertrande recalls the advice she has been given to drop the charges. Her anxiety about her situation intensifies and her health and sanity deteriorate as the landscape does (pp.75–82).

Structure

Key point

Information about the construction of the text provides supporting evidence for your interpretation of the novella. It is important to consider the effect of the structural elements of the text. Isolated information about the mechanics (such as the genre, style and structure) of the text is not meaningful until placed in the context of a broader analysis. Connect your observations about the construction of the text to your argument about what the text means.

The Wife of Martin Guerre is divided into four sections. The first chapter is the longest and relates the story of the marriage of Bertrande de Rols to Martin Guerre, followed by his disappearance and apparent return. It also tells of Bertrande's realisation that the man in her bed is not her husband, and follows the process she goes through to be rid of him and of the sin of adultery. This chapter most clearly resembles a conventional novel in its structure and style. It tells a fictionalised story of a young woman's development to maturity.

The second and third sections tell the narrative of the trial at Rieux and the appeal at the court of Toulouse. It becomes clearer in these sections that the novella was based upon a real trial. While it continues to be fictional, the text has a more formal and sparse style in these chapters. Dialogue is more prominent and reads in ways that suggest the text's source: a report of the legal process by one of the presiding judges. These chapters continue to focus on Bertrande's perspective and chart her mental and physical disintegration.

The final section, or 'Afterword', is outside the story of Bertrande de Rols but a significant aspect of the novella. It gives details of the process involved in the production of the text. It gives background to the trial not directly relevant to the fate of Bertrande de Rols, such as the execution of the judge whose report provided a record of proceedings. This section particularly allows stories and perspectives other than Bertrande's to emerge.

CHAPTER-BY-CHAPTER ANALYSIS

Chapter 1: Artigues (pp.5–13)

Summary: *Set in mountainous countryside in southern France in 1539. Marriage of Bertrande de Rols and Martin Guerre, both aged 11 years and children of feuding feudal families.*

The marriage: the individual vs. the community

This marriage takes place to mend the relationship between the village's two main families and to bring to both the advantages of an alliance. It is a dynastic marriage, common historically between wealthy families, in which the young couple are united for the benefits to the families of property and status. The wishes of the bride and groom are almost irrelevant to the proceedings. Individual preferences and romantic love were not major considerations in the sixteenth-century idea of marriage; they are modern concepts. '[T]he small bride received very little attention. After the first embraces and compliments, she sat beside her mother at the long table and ate the food which her mother served her from the big platters' (p.6).

The wedding follows a traditional format. After a marriage ceremony in church and celebratory meal the bride and groom are 'put to bed'. This ritual provides opportunity for the sexual union of the couple. In this case it is only symbolic because of the extreme youth and disinterest of the couple. It also refers to the marriage's purpose: the birth of children and the continuity of the dynasties. Rather than consummate the marriage, or even engage in conversation with each other, the couple sleep. The image of them sleeping suggests their lack of involvement in the proceedings.

This marriage, so significant in its intent, has no immediate effect because the two children are too young to live together. The next morning Bertrande returns to her mother's house. The eleven-year-old girl cannot at this point appreciate the meaning of her marriage. The strangeness of the situation is expressed in the observation that Bertrande 'found it quite as serious an affair as first communion' (p.6). Bertrande's recent first communion (a sacred ritual undertaken by young children as a sign of their religious commitment) was a serious affair but the consequences of her early marriage will be far graver.

The children are woken at midnight for the réveillon, a traditional bridal feast. It is brought to them by a servant who stays with the family throughout the story and becomes the seer, the voice of simple wisdom. '"Eat", said the woman, beaming upon them. "You have had all the rest of the affair – you may as well enjoy now your little feast, just the two of you"' (p.10). The maid comments on the peace and friendship that their marriage has brought to the village. Their marriage affects the happiness and stability of the whole community. This is a heavy responsibility for the young couple to bear. Bertrande is raised to attend to the collective good, and her marriage represents this. The story that unfolds in this text reveals the tension between individual and communal needs.

Key point

The first scene of the book is the marriage between the young children of wealthy feudal families. It establishes the priority of family and community in this society, and it explores the relationship between individual and collective needs. This is a theme that recurs throughout the text.

Q Much of the very first page is taken up with descriptions of the country. What do these communicate?

Q Why is the marriage of Bertrande de Rols and Martin Guerre the first scene in this novella?

Q What does the reader learn of the families involved in the wedding in the first pages?

Power

When Bertrande withdraws from the celebrations to a corner of the room, she finds Martin hiding there also. Bertrande has not spoken to him in all her life and had not known, until the day before, of the arrangement for them to marry. This is their first interaction. He greets her by 'cuff[ing] Bertrande soundly upon the ears, [he] scratched her face and pulled her hair' (pp.7–8). He does this 'in order to express his dislike of the affair, and also to express the power of his newly acquired sovereignty' (p.7). This response is most revealing about Martin's personality, his status in the family, his response to difficulty and his behaviour toward Bertrande.

Q What does the reader learn about the children from this scene?

The feudal system in which these children live gives total responsibility and authority to the head of the household – the *cap d'hostal*. When the bridal couple are put to bed, Bertrande realises that from now on she will be subject to the control of her father-in-law. He is an autocratic (sole ruler, from the Greek *autokrator*, derived from *auto* meaning 'self' and *kratos* meaning 'power') and harsh leader. Martin is his heir and stands to inherit his privileges: his property, his right to control it and other people, the loyalty of his household and the village, and the responsibilities for the care of others that his status involves. Martin's behaviour towards Bertrande suggests that he has learned his father's manner. Martin's gruffness becomes an identifying mark in the process of determining the real Martin Guerre.

The maid who brings the réveillon remarks that Martin is ugly but distinguished, with the potential to be a man of authority, like his father. She says Bertrande is pretty with lucky two-coloured eyes.

Q The maid/housekeeper has the function of seer in the text. What does her description of the bridal couple suggest about them and their fates?

Chapter 1: Artigues (pp.14–33)

Summary: *Bertrande becomes part of the Guerre household. She develops an affection for her husband and at twenty gives birth to an heir, Sanxi. Martin warns her that he must leave the farm for a week to avoid his father's wrath at his disobedience. Martin does not return.*

Agricultural life and the feudal system

When she is fourteen, Bertrande's mother dies and Bertrande goes to live with her husband at the Guerre family farm. She is guided around the farm, of which she will one day be mistress. The description of the farm is detailed and the reader can appreciate the labour necessary to produce sufficient food to maintain the household. Farm work is divided according to gender; Bertrande is put to work grinding meal while Martin labours in the fields. When the men return to the house after working, Monsieur Guerre is routinely offered warmed wine by his wife.

Q How does this ritual represent the power dynamics within the family?

Monsieur Guerre has both power and responsibility. The description of the farm and the life they lead suggests an uncertain existence. Bertrande observes on her first night that the farm, its animals and its inhabitants are safe because they are protected by Martin's father. 'Because of him the farm was safe, and therefore Artigues, and therefore Languedoc, and therefore France, and therefore the whole world was safe and as it should be' (p.17).The father is a severe man who 'rules' his household like a 'Homeric king'. (Homer is the author of two epic classical poems, the *Iliad* and the *Odyssey* and the word 'Homeric' is used here to refer to the immensity of Monsieur Guerre's power.) Monsieur Guerre is responsible for the safety and prosperity of his family and village. His bearing and manner reflect his power: 'he was in his own person both authority and security' (p.17).

According to custom and feudal law, Martin is subject to his father's authority until the father's death. He is given responsibility but no power or autonomy (permission to act for himself). He is legally a minor until that time when he, in turn, takes on the mighty responsibilities of *cap d'hostal*. At times, Martin resists his father's authority. Their relationship is expressed in the story of the bear hunt.

One day Martin joins a bear hunt without asking his father's permission. He returns triumphant with the bloody carcass of a bear. His father is angry that Martin had not asked for his permission to go hunting and hits him in the face, breaking two teeth. Bertrande is upset, but Martin says '"it was just"' (p.19). His mother explains to him, '"If you have no obedience for your father, your son will have none for you, and then what will become of the family? Ruin. Despair"' (p.19).

Martin seems to accept this harsh punishment for his disobedience and approves of the system that prevents him from being able to act for himself.

Q Why is Martin so accepting when he is punished severely by his father?

Love and abandonment

Gradually Bertrande develops respect and affection for Martin and an allegiance to him in his battles with his father. She develops a 'deep and joyous passion' (p.20) for her husband and at twenty becomes the mother to a son, Sanxi (p.20). As the mother to an heir, Bertrande's status in the family increases and her confidence grows.

One day Martin tells Bertrande that he is going away because he disobeyed his father by taking grain out of his father's grain store for planting in his own plot. He is convinced that he acts for the good of his family but knows his disobedience will be punished. Martin says he will be gone a week or so until his father's anger subsides. He does not return.

Key point

By leaving and then staying away Martin defies the feudal codes. He places his own desires above the needs of the community. He breaks faith with his wife. In her marriage and her role as wife, Bertrande contributes to the security and comfort of the community; by leaving, Martin avoids his responsibilities to her and to the household. He breaks with the terms of their marriage.

Martin abandons Bertrande just as she learns to love him, in the middle of her youthful radiance. She feels his absence greatly. The advantages of the union are diminished for her; she must bear greater responsibility and has less protection. She misses the intimacies and companionship of marriage.

The effect of Martin's absence on the household

The household becomes subdued after Martin leaves. One year after his disappearance Martin's mother dies. Four years after he leaves, his father is thrown from a horse and killed. His father's brother, Martin's Uncle Pierre, comes to manage the farm and the household. It is significant that the household unravels at the disappearance and disobedience of the heir. It suggests that the stability of the farm depends upon the maintenance of its feudal structure.

Ways of seeing

Bertrande's recollection of Martin becomes hazy. She is unclear about what he looked like and her mind plays tricks with her memories of him. Her mother-in-law earlier tells her that people remember things in different ways. Some '"do not remember with their eyes, but with their ears, maybe"' (p.30). She tells the young woman that she has a visual memory: '"I do not remember where [something] is, I see it"' (p.30). On one occasion Bertrande sees a man in the fields who she initially believes is Martin. When he comes close enough for Bertrande to see him clearly it is obviously not her husband. The man acknowledges her and goes on his way. She makes a journey to the town of Rieux to seek Martin out or hear word of him, and stays with her aunt. She becomes disoriented and thinks the sun 'rose in the west and shone through western windows all the morning' (p.33).

Key point

These moments of disorientation point to a larger theme about the ways in which perspective varies according to individual views or beliefs. The text calls attention to the significance and power of a particular point of view in various ways: in the contradictory views about du Tilh; in attempts to define Bertrande as mad to discredit her story; and in the legal process that weighs up conflicting opinion. In the text, truth seems elusive but conviction has a powerful material effect.

Bertrande's confusion about what she sees lays the foundation for a discussion about the ways in which particular perspectives or points of view are recognised and others undermined in the text.

Chapter 1: Artigues (pp.34–62)

Summary: *Arnaud du Tilh (posing as Martin) arrives home but Bertrande comes to believe that he is not the same man who left her eight years previously. She becomes pregnant to this man and her suspicions and concerns grow. Bertrande accuses him of being an impostor. He calms her and later, when she persists, calls her mad. He will not leave, so she reports him to the authorities to be rid of him and of her guilt at their sinful relationship.*

The relief of Martin's return and Bertrande's growing suspicion

Bertrande is relieved to be able to hand over to Martin his share of responsibilities and she 'surrendered herself to his love' (p.40). She 'rejoiced in the presence of this new Martin even more than in that of the old' and is soon pregnant (p.41). Sanxi is at first hesitant but soon becomes attached to the stranger. Du Tilh runs affairs successfully, is respectful of his servants and gentle with his family. The house becomes a happy home once more. It is precisely this peace and happiness that alerts Bertrande to Arnaud du Tilh's imposition upon them all.

Bertrande is suspicious from the first that this man is not her husband. When he arrives home Martin is familiar to Bertrande but more like 'a man who might have been Martin's ancestor but not young Martin Guerre' (p.35). Martin says to her '"Madame ... you are very beautiful"' (p.36). It is an uncharacteristic comment and a peculiar greeting from a man purporting to be her husband. Even on the night of his return she expresses her surprise at his arrival: '"I cannot believe it to be true"' (p.41).

During the pregnancy her sense that this man is not Martin Guerre increases. She is alarmed by this possibility and ready to blame herself for succumbing to him. Bertrande's concern about participating in the sin of adultery increases when she is pregnant. The pregnancy is evidence of her sin.

Adultery in sixteenth century France was regarded as a very great sin. It put into question the paternity and so legitimacy and inheritance of children. In an inheritance system determined through the male line, female adultery leads to confusion about property and power. The constancy and obedience of women was considered necessary for the stability of their way of life. Punishment for offenders was severe. Bertrande is also Catholic and the church forbade sexual relations between people not married to each other. So in spite of the pleasure of his company, and his satisfaction of her personal needs, Bertrande, a woman brought up to act for the communal good, rejects Arnaud du Tilh. To continue the relationship would mean transgressing against the laws of her society and placing herself in danger.

Key point

No matter what action she takes with respect to du Tilh it will be to her own disadvantage. Bertrande says of Arnaud du Tilh, '"I am imposed upon, deceived, betrayed into adultery, but not mad"' (p.47). It is also true that her position is difficult because she is imposed upon by her family, by the law and by the church.

Q Why are the other members of the Guerre household more easily able to accept the impostor as Martin Guerre?

Proving the truth, and the politics of madness

Bertrande becomes certain that du Tilh is not her husband and determined to prove that she has been betrayed. 'Although she had loved him passionately and joyously, and perhaps loved him still, and although he was the father of her son, she must rid herself of him' (p.47). She is not sure that she can prove her case and is concerned about the effect an unsuccessful lawsuit will have on her family. To test out the reaction to her beliefs she gently lets her sister-in-law know her thoughts. The sister strongly rejects the idea that Martin is an impostor and Bertrande is discouraged.

Evidence against du Tilh mounts and Bertrande goes, in great fear of the consequences, to the priest to confess. The priest also attempts to convince her that she is mistaken. It is convenient for him also that du Tilh remain in the village, for the priest and the impostor are friends. Although she is initially comforted by the priest's reassurance, Bertrande remains unconvinced that this man is Martin Guerre and continues to be disturbed. When she again becomes pregnant she says it is 'the burden of her sin made actual' (p.50), and this time cannot be convinced that her hormonal state is solely responsible for her continuing concern. Bertrande feels alienated from her own life and from those who owe her support. 'Familiar figures passed her, greeting her as they went on into the church. She answered them as in a dream, and as in a dream took the path to her farm. She felt like one who has been condemned to solitude, whether of exile or of prison' (p.50).

Q Why is no-one prepared to believe and support Bertrande?

Bertrande encourages du Tilh to leave again for the wars. To encourage him to go she denies she loves him, but he refuses to leave. "Can you suppose that while you believe this thing of me, I will ever leave you?" (p.52). This is a crucial mistake for Arnaud du Tilh as he misses this opportunity to leave in safety and Bertrande is forced, in the face of his persistence, to take severe action against him.

It is ironic, and central to the plot, that this man's kindness betrays him. '"It is not possible that this man should be Martin Guerre. For Martin Guerre, the son of the old master, proud and abrupt, like the old master, could never in the world speak so gaily to his own son. Ah! unhappy woman that I am, so to distrust the Good God who has sent me this happiness! I shall be punished. But this is also punishment in itself"' (pp.41–2). It is interesting that at this point she yearns for the real Martin, a gruff and harsh man, to return to free her from the persecution of the good-natured Arnaud du Tilh (p.52).

Q Why do you think Arnaud du Tilh refuses to leave Bertrande when she gives him warning of her conviction?

As Bertrande's health fails, from the stress of her situation, there comes startling evidence of du Tilh's guilt. Returning home from church, the family is approached by an old soldier who claims to have been Martin's friend. Not only does 'Martin' not recognise the man but the soldier claims that Martin lost his leg in battle, and concludes that du Tilh is a fraud. Bertrande, who does not witness this confrontation, is relieved to hear this evidence in support of her suspicions. Following this incident, Bertrande delivers a daughter who dies shortly after the birth. The priest arranges for the soldier's tale to be recorded and, after his account is given to Bertrande, her health and vitality return.

Key point

Bertrande insists that this man is not her husband. However, her family have faith in him and they need him. They are angry at Bertrande for unsettling the certainty of his identity and so the contentment of their lives. Du Tilh encourages the notion that she is mad because it is important to discredit her claims. This is effective: her family believe her mentally unstable and her story carries no weight. This demonstrates the way in which the more powerful can influence what is accepted as 'true'.

Arnaud tells the priest that Bertrande asked him to leave her and that he had refused because he believed that to leave would '"confirm her in this madness, and that I should be deserting her to years of pain – as if I were to fasten upon her the guilt of a sin"' (p.59). The priest advises Martin to leave for a few days to let Bertrande recover from her fragile and distressed state. Du Tilh approaches Uncle Pierre for money Martin entrusted to him in his youth. When he discovers that the money is no longer available, du Tilh is angry.

Bertrande enlists the help of Pierre Guerre who comes to believe her story. With his support she determines to press her point. When she learns that du Tilh attempted to leave, her response expresses both pain and relief. '"He wishes money in hand in order to leave us. Now that he fears detection, now that he has pillaged us, now that he has almost killed me, he will go away"' (p.61). While she desires to be rid of him and free of the guilt of adultery, she is sad to have to do this because she loved him and he cared for her. She also understands that her family needs him.

Q What does Bertrande's decision to pursue prosecution of the 'new' Martin, despite her misgivings, reveal about her values and character?

As he refuses to leave, Bertrande must pursue her belief and have him arrested. She is symbolically '[s]tanding beside the master's chair, before the hearth' (p.61) when she accuses the man, now bound in chains and accompanied by guards, of being an impostor. The household watches in astonishment as du Tilh leaves and Bertrande stands, eyes toward the hearth, feeling 'entirely alone' (p.62).

Key point

Bertrande is alone again as the man, who has given her both pleasure and pain, is led away. She is again cast in the role of abandoned wife – an experience she previously endured following Martin Guerre's departure – and is again left to assume the responsibilities of the estate and household.

Chapter 2: Rieux

Summary: *The trial takes place in Rieux. Jean Espagnol and others come forward with evidence against the prisoner. The judges condemn him to death.*

Symbols of disorientation

Bertrande's complaint against Arnaud du Tilh is made at Rieux and, when she goes there to attend court, she stays with her aunt. On her previous visit it seemed to her that the sun rose in the west. This time the sun 'shone from the east, as it should do, and Bertrande marvelled that she had ever felt confused about the direction' (p.63). Bertrande draws a parallel between this clarity about the direction of the sun and her certainty that this man is not her husband. They have both been issues that confused her that now seem plainly obvious.

Q What is the significance of Bertrande's confusion about the sun?

Women and the law

During the trial, Bertrande's evidence consists of seemingly trivial things that make the judges smile condescendingly. She overhears spectators condemning her for remaining with du Tilh for three years after she discovered him to be an impostor. She finds her character under scrutiny in a trial in which she herself is the accuser.

Jean Espagnol testifies that the prisoner is Arnaud du Tilh (otherwise known as Pansette – this name means 'the belly', and obviously refers to his appetites). His evidence against du Tilh is compelling and supported by others. Espagnol claims that Arnaud du Tilh told him previously that he was masquerading as Martin Guerre, who had earlier sold him the rights to his estate and the right to impersonate him.

Bertrande cannot believe this evidence. Such a deal reduces her to a piece of property, able to be bought and sold at whim by her husband. It suggests that Martin Guerre has little regard for her welfare or happiness, and makes her concern for his family's honour a sad sacrifice of herself. Bertrande's struggle to rid herself of the man she once loved shows misplaced loyalty to the interests of the Guerre family and their household. She gives allegiance to a husband who has no regard for her, and who appears to have sold the rights to her affection and her body. In effect, she has been campaigning not for her own happiness but for the rights and honour of a man who has discarded her.

The judges convict Arnaud du Tilh and condemn him to death. Bertrande, whose aim has been to be rid of his presence only, is horrified at the sentence. '"Not death! Not death! No, no, I have not demanded his death!"' (p.69). Bertrande brings the complaint to establish that this man is not her husband, but has no desire for retribution and even questions Pierre Guerre's request for money.

Bertrande mistakenly believes that the law does her bidding and is shocked when the punishment decided upon is so much harsher than she would wish it to be. Bertrande fails to understand that the law regards his crimes against her as crimes against society as a whole. Hence, the punishment is decided by the court, rather than according to that which would satisfy her alone.

Key point

Bertrande is imposed upon by authorities who act for her but without regard for the complexity of her feelings for du Tilh. She would not have him executed. In the legal context, du Tilh's sins are considered significant because his actions are regarded as a serious threat to the whole community. The text suggests that the law is determined by people in power to protect their interests. Arnaud du Tilh's actions challenge the feudal society and are severely punished.

Bertrande's horror upon hearing the sentence is greeted by the prisoner with joy. Despite the prospect of execution he seems to be pleased with this demonstration of Bertrande's continued affection.

Chapter 3: Toulouse

Summary: *Martin's sisters appeal the decision. The priest tells Bertrande to reconsider. She refuses and there is a second trial in Toulouse. The judges decide in favour of the defendant, Arnaud du Tilh. Then the real Martin Guerre appears and the decision is reversed.*

Truth

Martin's sisters believe that this man is Martin Guerre with such conviction that they bring about an appeal of the judgement against him. Bertrande considers withdrawing her charges and she is begged to do so by most of the village. She agrees that she does not wish Arnaud du Tilh to die. '"It is no more than just to remember that he has been kind to us – kind to all, save me, and kind even to me after a strange fashion"' (p.71). First the priest, the representative of the God she believes will condemn and punish her, counsels her to withdraw the charges. He does so to prevent the consequences of an unjust execution and to protect those who will be hurt by it.

Q Read Bertrande's conversation with the priest (pp.71–2). Why does he try to convince Bertrande to withdraw charges against Arnaud du Tilh?

The youngest sister also attempts to discourage Bertrande from continuing with her cause. She is still convinced that the man is her brother, and an admired and respected leader whose absence would end the family's happiness. The sister emphasises the pleasure that Arnaud du Tilh has brought to her family. Only Bertrande is implicated in the sin of adultery, with its heavy punishment and stigma; the rest of the household is able to enjoy his presence without compromising themselves. Bertrande says she cannot deny the truth. '"It is only the truth for you, not for us," returned the weeping girl' (p.73).

Bertrande appeals to the housekeeper, the servant who had so long ago brought the young couple their midnight feast. She tells Bertrande she '"would have you still be deceived. We were all happy then"' (p.75). This implies that she acknowledges some truth in Bertrande's claim but wishes it were possible to go on regardless. Bertrande responds to the housekeeper as she did to her sister-in-law, that is, with an appeal to truth. '"The truth is only the truth. I cannot change it, if I would"' (p.75).

Key point

Bertrande believes in truth. Her aim is to have the courts recognise her perspective as truth. As the narrative focuses on the trials, the idea of truth becomes problematic. Each trial presents many different opinions on the identity of the defendant. Twice the courts rule against Bertrande's view and against the truth.

Bertrande waivers not because she changes her mind about the man's identity but because she questions the wisdom of pressing her point, for she, too, fears the consequences of her actions. '"I did not demand his death," she reminded herself; "but now I must demand it"' (p.72). She is still convinced that the man is Arnaud du Tilh and that she needs to be rid of him to be rid of her sin.

It is also possible to read Bertrande's actions as a defiant stand to assert herself as an individual. Bertrande has been imposed upon by all around her, particularly by the men she trusts. She has been limited by her family, by the priest, by Martin and du Tilh. She is given no opportunity for self-determination. Rather than looking at her appeal to the authorities as a pointless and limiting action, it is possible to interpret her legal suit as a rare and bold expression of defiance or independence. When she decides to continue with the appeal, she does so knowing that, if found guilty, du Tilh will die. This may represent a glorious triumph for Bertrande and her 'solitary justice' (p.92).

Q What do you think of the idea that Bertrande is motivated to proceed with the appeal out of anger at those who have oppressed her? Can this idea be supported by the text?

Dying doves

The housekeeper kills and plucks doves for cooking as she speaks, and Bertrande empathises with the bird as she watches its life and blood run out of it. She watches, 'feeling her own strength drop slowly away like the blood of the dove' (p.75). Like the bird, Bertrande's vitality has been sapped. Her strength and optimism are gone. Like the bird, her life is in the hands of others; first of her family who give her in marriage to Martin Guerre at the age of eleven; then of Martin who abandons her; then of Arnaud du Tilh who deceives her; and then the judiciary who take over her cause and choose execution as the impostor's punishment.

The dead doves lie in a 'pile of soft grey-feathered bodies' (p.74) on the table. Bertrande's identification with the dying dove suggests a reference to the frustrated possibilities – the dead ends – of her life. Perhaps the image refers to Arnaud's death. It may even refer to Bertrande and Arnaud's dead baby girl. Ultimately, the image expresses Bertrande's distress and oppression.

The journey to Toulouse

Travelling to Toulouse for the appeal, Bertrande remembers that in her mind she travelled this journey with Martin when he first left home. The image of her riding slowly to the trial haunted by a memory of her husband suggests the extent to which her actions are determined by him in his absence.

Q Why does Martin's memory motivate her to pursue this course against Arnaud du Tilh?

Riding to Toulouse, Bertrande observes Pierre Guerre riding in front of her. She sees his 'broad and honest back going steadily on' (p.77). He is for her a figure of continuity and solidity that she associates with the local tradition and way of life. Pierre Guerre is the 'one remaining defender of the old authority of her husband's house … He was for her that day a tradition more potent than the church. In her country the church had sometimes been denied, but … [it] had never denied the tradition of which Pierre Guerre was the symbol' (pp.77–8). It is partly out of duty to this tradition, and to Martin's authority within it, that she proceeds with her cause.

Riding to Toulouse she again contemplates withdrawing the charges. While she is keen to return to a time of happiness, supported by those who love her, she knows that if she were to withdraw charges against du Tilh she could not accept herself. She knows that the pleasure brought to others would cost her conscience dearly. She considers her feelings if the court in Toulouse were to reverse the decision. She knows she will never believe that this man is her husband, but she wonders if the authority of the judges, and so the king and so God, will enable her to receive Arnaud du Tilh as her husband again.

Bertrande recalls various conversations she has had that contribute to her confusion. She remembers the advice of the priest, her sister-in-law and the housekeeper. In the narrative, these conversations are juxtaposed against each other and test Bertrande's will.

The journey is accompanied by much anxiety as Bertrande considers the various perspectives on the case. As she approaches the courtroom she becomes ill. She fears committing an even more serious sin than that of adultery. She knows that du Tilh will be executed if his guilt is confirmed by this court. She worries particularly about not taking the priest's advice.

Religious tension

On their journey to Toulouse, Pierre Guerre and Bertrande stay overnight at an inn. During dinner they hear conversation about the recent massacre of Catholics by Protestants in Amboise. This hints at the high state of tension, on religious grounds, that existed at the time. Pierre Guerre, also a devout Catholic, is shocked at the bloodshed, which is threatening the peace and stability of the society.

It is interesting to find reference to religious conflicts and political struggles in the text, just at the point at which the appeal begins. The violent conflict between competing ideologies strengthens the idea that the truth is not absolute but subjective (that is, dependent on the individual). As referred to in the text, Protestants and Catholics are each battling to assert their truth as a certainty. Ultimately, however, these truths are not 'provable' principles, but matters of belief and faith.

Key point

The discussion in the inn about events at Amboise disturbs Bertrande, who is already agitated by what she regards as her responsibility to expose the truth. Its placement in the text draws attention to a parallel between the legal process, with its dependence on subjective evidence for determining the truth, and religious faith, which justifies war as a means of proving the superiority of a certain belief. Both institutions – law and religion – appear to be founded on subjective or unprovable truths, which can have real and devastating consequences. In each instance referred to in the text in which ideas of truth are in conflict, the result is death.

After hearing of the massacre in Amboise, Bertrande concludes that she must proceed with her case '[f]or the sake of a truth, to free myself from a deceit which was consuming and killing me' (p.81). She also recalls the discussion she had with her sister-in-law about her need to prove the truth, and her sister-in-law's response that, '"It is true only for you"' (p.81).

The appeal

Pierre and Bertrande are questioned separately. They each feel isolated and intimidated by the procedure. The authority of the law works on them. They are peasants from an isolated village visiting a large, established town for a court case in which a person's life hangs in the balance. Pierre is laughed at for being countrified and unsophisticated. At Rieux he is known and respected, so his testimony there has greater weight. After his interview he returns to their lodgings with the feeling that his poor performance has threatened their case.

Evidence in this trial includes the shoemaker's testimony that Arnaud du Tilh's foot is smaller than that of Martin Guerre's. Other physical evidence favours the accused: identical broken teeth, scars, eyes, a nail missing, warts.

In support of Bertrande is Carbon Bareau, maternal uncle of Arnaud du Tilh. In an emotional state, he claims the prisoner is Arnaud du Tilh. '"[H]e has a way with him, a way of stealing the heart, but I have feared for him ever since he grew old enough to talk. He has had no respect for the laws ... he has even declared there is no God ... With no faith, no respect for family, nor the law of the kingdom, what could one hope for"' (p.85). This is an important description of du Tilh and it supports the idea that he is punished for breaking the laws of society and of God.

Q To what extent do you think the uncle's description of Arnaud du Tilh is accurate?

Arnaud's brothers also say the prisoner 'resembled' their brother (p.85). It is very hard for them to denounce their brother when to do so will lead to his death, and they will not commit themselves. Evidence for each case mounts. The housekeeper gives her evidence by way of a story about the prisoner knowing just how and where she stored certain underwear.

The judges ultimately decide that the prisoner is Martin Guerre. As those in the courtroom relax after this judgement and the clerk prepares to enter the verdict in the records, a scruffy soldier is admitted amid much noise. He carries a halberd (combined spear and battleaxe) as do the soldiers who accompany him into the courtroom. His stance is aggressive. He tells the judges, '"I am without any doubt Martin Guerre … I lost my leg before St Quentin in the year fifty-seven. I am the father of Sanxi Guerre, and of no other children"' (p.88).

Nothing has been known of Martin Guerre for many years. This brief introduction reveals several interesting pieces of information.

- His presence is proof that he is alive. Bertrande had been convinced that her husband was murdered by Arnaud du Tilh. She could not believe that her husband remained alive and left her deliberately unprotected and unsupported.
- The information that he lost a leg in battle reveals that rather than having been killed, Martin has been roaming the country as a soldier of fortune. This was a time of war and there was need for soldiers to fight. It makes it clear that Martin did indeed abandon Bertrande and Sanxi and his responsibilities to the farm.
- By stating that he is the father of Sanxi Guerre only, Martin puts emphasis not on Arnaud's impersonation of him and deception of Bertrande, but on Bertrande's accidental adultery. This is the interpretation on events that Bertrande herself fears. It makes Bertrande responsible for the situation. Rather than understanding that Bertrande has been imposed upon, Martin blames her for participating in adultery.

Bertrande is summoned to appear before both Martin Guerre and Arnaud du Tilh. She recognises and addresses Martin:

> My dear lord and husband, at last you are returned. Pity me and forgive me, for my sin was occasioned only by my great desire for your presence, and surely, from the hour wherein I knew I was deceived, I have laboured with all the strength of my soul to rid myself of the destroyer of my honour and my peace (p.90).

The court is apologetic and sympathetic, but Martin's response is cold.

> Dry your tears, Madame. They cannot, and they ought not, move my pity. The example of my sisters and my uncle can be no excuse for you, Madame, who knew me better than any living soul. The error into which you plunged could only have been caused by wilful blindness. You, and you only, Madame, are answerable for the dishonour which has befallen me (p.91).

Key point

If there is any doubt about Martin Guerre's identity, the nature of this response confirms it. He is harsh, authoritarian and self-centred in his first words to his wife. His behaviour conforms with Bertrande's expectations of him. It is reminiscent of his father's own style and of the treatment Bertrande received from Martin before he disappeared. Bertrande 'gazed steadily into the face of her husband and seemed there to see the countenance of the old Monsieur, the patriarch whose authority had been absolute over her youth and over that of the boy who had been her young husband' (p.91). His behaviour is a sure mark of his identity.

The way he condemns his wife is revealing: his concern is for his honour. According to Martin and to contemporary values, in taking a man other than her husband to bed, Bertrande has disregarded Martin's ownership of and exclusive right to his wife's body.

Martin accuses Bertrande of *deliberately* dishonouring him. His emphasis is upon the insult he believes he has received through her disobedience. He blames her for what the narrative demonstrates was unintended adultery. He regards the situation solely from his own perspective. He does not consider his responsibilities as a husband, but is anxious to remind Bertrande of hers as a wife. No apology or explanation is offered for his absence. Martin makes himself the centre of the story when in fact, as Lewis suggests by the title, this story is about his wife, Bertrande de Rols.

The devotion of Arnaud du Tilh

In the final courtroom scene, Arnaud du Tilh reveals something of himself for the first time. He acknowledges that he was captivated by Bertrande and reformed by her. When addressed by him in the courtroom, Bertrande is scathing in return. Arnaud asks for her pity and intervention, but she refuses.

> "You had no mercy upon me, either upon body or upon soul," replied Bertrande.
>
> "Then, Madame," said du Tilh, and there was at last neither arrogance nor levity in his voice, "I can but die by way of atonement" (p.92).

While awaiting execution he signs a full confession. He states that he had often been mistaken for Martin Guerre and sought to take advantage of this to steal money. He was inspired to join the household by Bertrande's 'beauty and grace'. She caused the 'rogue' to become 'for three long years an honest man' (p.91).

Key point

Arnaud is convicted of the crimes of 'imposture, falsehood, substitution of name and person, adultery, rape, sacrilege, plagiat, which is the detention of a person who properly belongs to another, and of larceny' (pp.92–3). He has transgressed against the proper order of things and for this he must die. He will be executed symbolically outside the home he improperly claimed as his own. (Zemon Davis tells us that the original report states that du Tilh was only convicted of 'imposture and false supposition of name and person and of adultery.' Judge Jean de Coras added a number of crimes to the conviction in his report.)

Bertrande's isolation

Following her conversation with du Tilh, Bertrande leaves the courtroom. She does not see the crowd as it parts to let her pass. She leaves alone, finally free of the imposition of du Tilh and of the burden of an imaginary Martin.

> Leaving the love which she had rejected because it was forbidden, and the love which had rejected her, she walked through a great emptiness to the door, and so on into the streets of Toulouse, knowing that the return of Martin Guerre would in no measure compensate for the death of Arnaud, but knowing herself at last free, in her bitter, solitary justice, of both passions and of both men (p.92).

Isolation and loneliness are again Bertrande's fate. This conclusion is particularly bitter and ironic because the story suggests that Bertrande is betrayed by the same traditions, laws and customs that she seeks to uphold. Bertrande has behaved consistently within the morality of her society and acted according to the laws forbidding adultery, yet her attempts to free herself from sin are largely unsupported and she is left suffering from a court case that ought to have left her free and triumphant. She receives little support from her family, her church, the court, or the waiting crowds.

Q What does 'solitary justice' mean?

Chapter 4: Afterword

Summary: *Contains details of the original case notes from the trial and news of the death of the author of this report. It also discusses the history of interest in the trial and gives some information about the production of* The Wife of Martin Guerre.

History of the story of Bertrande de Rols and Martin Guerre

Towards the end of the narrative it becomes clearer that this case originates from an actual account of a judicial trial. The author shows this through the language and expressions used. There are increasing references to the trial, and the dialogue begins to read like a transcript.

In the final section of the text, details are given of the record of the case by Jean de Coras, Judge of Toulouse. His account of the trial with his own notes was published in Paris in 1565.

Lewis did not use this source in her preparations for the text but consulted other secondary materials. From these she reconstructed the story of Bertrande de Rols and Martin Guerre. The novella builds on the information given at the trial.

Q What effect does this information about the original trial report have on your understanding of *The Wife of Martin Guerre*?

The 'Afterword' provides information about the public response to the trial. It was a notorious case that attracted widespread interest from the date of the original trial up until today. French lawyer and author Michel de Montaigne was present in the courtroom when the sentence was passed. In his writings he suggested that the evidence was inconclusive, and that legal reform was necessary. He called for the invention of a general judgement that would allow courts to rule that they could not actually decide the case (p.95). Estienne Pasquier, who also lived at the time of the trial, was ready to condemn Martin Guerre for his treatment of his wife and suggested punishing him also (p.95). This suggests that the notion of the husband holding complete power over his wife did not go unquestioned at the time, nor did the obvious unfairness of her situation.

Representation

As the 'Afterword' shows, *The Wife of Martin Guerre* is the fictionalisation of real events. Remember, the novella takes as one of its themes the nature of truth. This includes reference to the process of representation that the text itself is involved in. It forces the reader to consider whether the story accurately represents the story of Bertrande de Rols and the trial of Arnaud du Tilh. The process of translation, interpretation and fictionalisation involved in a project such as this will only represent one interpretation of the reality. Natalie Zemon Davis' historical exploration of the trial differs greatly from the novella, and it is worth reading not only for its historical information but also because it shows that different representations or accounts of the same event will contain different 'truths'.

Q Is it wise or desirable or even possible to represent this story accurately?

Point of view

The novella engages with ideas about the nature of representation, perspective and truth. These ideas are explored in various ways in the text: in what has been referred to as Bertrande's disorientation; as Bertrande wrestles with the advice of those around her; in the narrator's references to the subjectivity of truth; in the narrative's sympathy for Bertrande de Rols rather than the men involved in the case; in the relationship between the fiction of the novella and the fact of the trial.

That a trial was the inspiration for the text makes sense of these concerns. A legal trial is the negotiation of a contentious issue. Its purpose is to make sense of, or decide between, various perspectives on the same events. A legal procedure depends upon a difference of opinion. Without conflict there is no need for a trial. Including information about the trial and its documentation makes sense of the novella and its themes.

The judge

Coras was not only Judge of the Court at Toulouse but also Chancellor of Queen Marguerite of Navarre and a devout Protestant. He was murdered in provincial riots that followed the St Bartholomew's Day Massacre in Paris. His corpse, dressed in robes of office, was hung from an elm tree in the courtyard of the building that housed the courts.

Q What purpose does this information about Jean de Coras serve in terms of understanding the text?

CHARACTERS & RELATIONSHIPS

Bertrande de Rols

Key quotes

'"... she has the lucky eyes, the two-coloured eyes, brown and green, and the lucky people bring luck to those they love"' (p.10).

'He had deserted her in the full beauty of her youth, in the height of her great passion, he had shamed her and wounded her' (p.27).

'She enclosed in her heart a single fierce determination, and outwardly her life went on as usual' (p.53).

'She was entirely alone' (p.62).

Bertrande de Rols is the main character of the novella *The Wife of Martin Guerre*. The title makes clear that the dramatic focus of the story is not the trial, but the feelings and dilemmas of the abandoned wife. The third-person limited perspective means that events are viewed from the point of view of Bertrande. The reader learns about Bertrande and about the world she lives in.

Bertrande's character is revealed as she struggles with the pressures and dilemmas that face her. The story begins with Bertrande's marriage at the age of eleven and tells of her settling into the world of her husband and his family. She establishes relationships in this world and finds security and peace within the structures of traditional feudal farming life. When her husband Martin disappears, Bertrande must manage the household on her own. She does so with composure and skill. After many years, a changed Martin, a gentle, considered and loving man, returns to her. The deepening conviction that this man is not the real Martin Guerre unsettles her. She battles with her conscience about living with a man who is not her husband.

Obedience

Bertrande is motivated in her struggle to be rid of Arnaud by a sense that she must behave in accordance with the values and rules of her community and of the institutions that regulate her daily life. Church and family place expectations on her to behave in certain ways. This is particularly so because she is a woman of an era in which females held very little power as individuals.

Bertrande is patient in the face of the many pressures on her: she is married at an early age to a boy she does not know; she obeys his father; she is abandoned by her husband; she is deceived by a man pretending to be her husband; she is defined as mad when she tells the truth; and her pursuit of justice is taken over by the courts.

There is considerable pressure on Bertrande to accept the false Martin. When finally she takes her cause to the courts it is because she fears she will be punished by Martin and by God if she does not reject the impostor. When Martin reappears he condemns her unreasonably for ever believing that Arnaud du Tilh was her husband.

It is ironic and unjust that Bertrande's quest to be rid of Arnaud and to have the truth determined gives her neither satisfaction nor justice. This is a reminder that Bertrande does not act for her personal happiness but in order to live in harmony with her community's expectations.

Q What has been achieved by the end of the trial process?

Q Whose interests have been served by the verdict?

Key point

Ultimately, there is no victory for Bertrande despite having the truth of her accusation proved. She is made neither happy nor comfortable by the appearance of the true Martin Guerre.

Anger

It is possible to understand Bertrande as either a victim of the institutions that govern her everyday life, or as an angry woman seeking justice.

Bertrande has been abandoned and imposed upon by men she has trusted. She feels betrayed by Martin but is aware that, if he ever returns, his inherited authority would make it 'improper' for her to complain (p.27).

She is certainly angry with Arnaud du Tilh for his betrayal and his refusal to leave. She is still prepared to acknowledge that he was good to her and that she was fond of him. When it appears that he will leave, Bertrande weeps (p.61). When he is sentenced to death she cries out against the verdict.

Q How much is anger a motivation for Bertrande? Is obedience a greater factor?

Q What does Bertrande seek when she refers her case to the courts?

Many of the people around Bertrande pressure her as she tries to decide what to do. While she fears being punished by God for adultery, her priest tells her to trust Martin. Martin's sisters are sure Bertrande is mistaken and believe she is mad for pursuing her cause. She is motivated by a sense of duty toward the absent Martin and by concern for his family's honour. She turns to the law to rid herself of Arnaud du Tilh but is wracked with doubt when it becomes evident that to pursue this course will result in his death.

Throughout her difficulties Bertrande remains focused on behaving in a way that she thinks of as right, in spite of the conflicting advice she receives. She begins to disintegrate physically and emotionally as the people in her community pressure her to accept Arnaud. The whole process leaves her worn out. The final image has her departing with dignity from the courtroom untouched by the crowd and utterly alone.

It is valuable to allow both interpretations of Bertrande's motivation to stand. Much of the interest in the text arises out of the complexities of her situation. It is not clear to Bertrande what is the right action for her to take with respect to Arnaud du Tilh. She is certainly imposed upon.

She is also a woman of some strength and, although very patient, she has cause for anger.

Loneliness

Bertrande is repeatedly described as lonely or alone. Bertrande's loneliness shows her increasing distance from those around her. Her pursuit of justice drives her from the affection of her family. The priest's opposition to her position means that she does not have the aid of the church. Her faith in the legal system's ability to act for her in administering justice is questioned.

In the final scene of the novella, Bertrande is weary and alone. She is 'at last free, in her bitter, solitary justice, of both passions and of both men' (p.92). Her decisions have been guided by her personal sense of what is right. They have been made against the advice of her loved ones and have cost her contentment and security. She is alone because she decides that it is important to have her truth publicly recognised. This difficult process ironically distances her from the very institutions that she sought to defend: the family and the church.

Bertrande's pursuit of justice is motivated by her need to behave well within the rules and conventions of her society. She seeks to clear herself of the momentous crime of adultery that, at the time, attracted social, religious and legal punishment of the heaviest kind. She has been raised to observe the rules of her feudal community and has to this point conformed. Bertrande is a woman of her time and the alternative, of remaining knowingly with a man not her husband, is not a real option. In spite of all of this she acts alone, against much opposition and with great bravery. When the trial is finished 'hate and love have together exhausted the soul' of Bertrande (p.93).

Martin Guerre

Key quotes

'He had disliked being married, and, in order to express his dislike of the affair, and also to express the power of his newly acquired sovereignty, he cuffed Bertrande soundly upon the ears, scratched her face and pulled her hair, all without a word' (pp.7–8).

'Martin resembled his father greatly, both physically and in disposition' (p.21).

'Outwardly, Martin had the swarthy skin, the high forehead, the grey eyes, the flat, short nose, the lips, the high cleft chin of his father, and something of his father's build. Too early labour at the plough had rounded his shoulders. Nevertheless he was a skilful swordsman and boxer, agile, tall, and well-developed for his years ... His ugliness was ancestral, and that in itself was good' (p.22).

'"He had in him, it is true, the qualities of a great man"' (p.71).

Martin Guerre is the husband of the novella's main character, Bertrande de Rols. While his name appears in the title and he is an important figure in the text, his significance is greater in his absence than in his presence.

Martin is a coarse and rough young man before he leaves and savage when he returns. In spite of his harshness and disinterest, his wife is bound to honour him by the tradition that gives him, as her husband, authority over her. She must attend to his interests while he is absent. She looks after his farm and cares for his family. Her pursuit of justice – her attempt to be rid of du Tilh and to be cleared of the guilt of adultery – is motivated by her obligation to Martin. Martin's authority haunts the whole story in spite of his physical absence.

> He had deserted her in the full beauty of her youth, in the height of her great passion, he had shamed her and wounded her, and when he returned, if he should return after the death of his father, his authority would be as great as his father's then was, and to murmur against his treatment of her would then be improper in the highest degree. (p.27)

Martin rejects his inheritance

Martin's relationship with his father is fraught. Martin appears, at least initially, to participate willingly in the feudal culture into which he is born (p.19). Within this system everyone and everything in the household is ruled by the patriarch. Martin's father is autocratic and punishes disobedience harshly. Martin understands that his obedience is necessary for the security of the farm and family, and that it will be rewarded when he in turn inherits the position of *cap d'hostal*.

Q When Martin is punished by his father for bear-hunting without his permission, Bertrande declares the punishment unjust; her husband and his mother find it just; and no-one complains to Monsieur Guerre. Explain.

As he matures, Martin takes on responsibility for the farm but has no autonomy. He begins to defy his father. He leaves to escape punishment for taking extra grain from his father's store to plant in his own fields. By staying away he not only avoids his father's anger but also rejects the traditional way of life.

Key point

When he does not return, Martin rejects his privileged place in the strictly defined structure of the feudal system. As the only son, Martin stands to inherit his father's position. Martin has an advantage of power within this system that his sisters and his wife can never have.

Q Janet Lewis demonstrates that the feudal system provided society with figures of authority and security (p.17). In gaining this, what did people lose? What do Martin and Bertrande gain and lose by obedience to the system?

By staying away Martin also rejects responsibility for his wife. If we remember that their relationship was forged not for love but mutual convenience and obligation, Martin's departure is a betrayal of the terms of their commitment. When he remains absent, Martin rejects the ancient feudal structures that regulated everyday life. He places his own comfort ahead of the needs of his community.

Q Why did Bertrande and Martin marry? What were the advantages and disadvantages of arranged marriage?

The defining mark of Martin's identity

Martin returns and appears in the courtroom at Toulouse at the eleventh hour. He responds to Bertrande's plea for forgiveness with 'perfect coldness' (p.91). This severity confirms that he is the real Martin Guerre. His manner is the defining mark of his identity. Arnaud du Tilh's gentleness distinguished him from the gruff Martin Guerre and confirmed Bertrande's suspicion that he was not her husband. This is the tragedy of Bertrande's quest. To quiet her conscience Bertrande seeks to be rid of a man who is kind to her and to return to one who is not.

Arnaud du Tilh

Key quotes

'"I thought that to leave her then would but confirm her in this madness, and that I should be deserting her to years of pain – as if I were to fasten upon her the guilt of a sin"' (p.59).

'The prisoner had started also at Bertrande's cry. In spite of the sentence just passed upon him, his eyes were clear, and his face bright, one would have said, with joy' (p.69).

'"Can you not marvel now that the rogue, Arnaud du Tilh, for your beauty and grace, became for three long years an honest man?"' (p.91).

'There was no soul in my parish of Artigues who did not benefit in some way from his presence here' (p.71).

'"He has had no respect for the laws, gentlemen. It breaks my heart to say that he has even declared there is no God. He has revered his parents not at all. With no faith, no respect for family, nor the law of the kingdom, what could one hope for, gentlemen? He has a good heart, that is all. But what is a good heart when he can so disgrace an honourable family?"' (p.85).

Arnaud du Tilh is the man who impersonates Martin Guerre. The reader, however, learns little of du Tilh himself. He remains unknown. What is revealed comes through the trial and at the very end by way of the confession he signs while in prison awaiting execution (p.92). The narrative is largely limited to Bertrande's perspective and while this means the reader is not given the point of view of du Tilh, it allows us to participate in Bertrande's delight at his presence *and* her ultimate frustration.

Du Tilh is well-spoken, gentle and kind. These positive characteristics distinguish him from the real Martin Guerre. His likeability becomes the mark of his deceit. When he is uncharacteristically short with her, Bertrande remarks, '"He has profited well from my complaints, this impostor"' (p.52). There is much resistance to Bertrande's lawsuit because this man's behaviour has benefited so many. Sanxi's relationship with him is positive, the household is happy and the farm runs successfully. The village is advantaged as well. The priest trusts him and considers him an advisor.

Despite appearing to be 'good', du Tilh's transgressions are many. He seduces Bertrande, manipulates her, and turns her family against her. He convinces the village that she is mad. He persists in his deception even when he sees the damage it does her. He lies, and is cunning and sneaky. He continues the pretence until Martin appears and it is impossible for du Tilh to deny his deception.

Q Why does the reader feel sympathy for the man who deceives Bertrande to the point of madness and physical disintegration?

When Carbon Bareau testifies at Toulouse against du Tilh, his description of his nephew's beliefs is greatly disturbing to the court. Du Tilh is said to deny the authority of religion, family, and the king. In doing so he challenges the conventions that supported sixteenth century French society. He is convicted of, among other crimes, adultery, sacrilege and plagiat. These are serious offences against the social institutions of marriage, the church, and even property law.

The impostor becomes the hero

Janet Lewis makes Arnaud du Tilh into an idealised figure. She introduces him into her version of events as a kind man who shows great generosity and gentleness as the head of the household. He treasures Bertrande and is moved by his love for her. Nothing in contemporary reports of the trial suggests that this was the case but Lewis's interpretation gives her novella a dramatic structure and an historically appropriate reference to the medieval romance tradition. (Medieval or chivalric romances feature an ideal knight who acts under a strict moral code of courage and courtesy. Chivalrous knights pay passionate but platonic homage to a courtly woman.)

Key point

The novella draws on the romance genre, with Arnaud du Tilh, the deceitful wanderer, reformed through the redemptive power of love into an honest and noble man. He becomes the novella's hero and gives it irony and pathos (a quality that evokes sadness or pity). That he makes Bertrande and her family happy complicates the moral issues that confront her. For she must sacrifice him and her personal happiness to uphold the moral code in which she believes.

How du Tilh manages deceit

When he first arrives in the village, du Tilh is approached by Pierre Guerre as he walks away from the Guerre house. This suggests that he either hesitates and retreats from impersonating Martin or that his technique is to allow those that know Martin to lead the deceit (pp.39–40). The first meeting with Bertrande is also revealing about how he manages the deceit. The false Martin learnt about life in Artigues from the real Martin Guerre. Primarily he takes his cues from those around him and need initiate nothing (p.35). Du Tilh becomes skilled at gathering information about people from general conversation. He uses all of this to build knowledge about Martin Guerre's world and to negotiate his way around it. This is confirmed in his confession.

The housekeeper

The housekeeper is present throughout the whole story; she is the maid who brings the young couple their réveillon on their wedding night, and the senior domestic servant by the time Bertrande inherits responsibility for the household. This woman functions as a seer who reveals wisdom and truth. Her comments illuminate ideas and inform the reader. Bertrande respects her and considers her a significant member of the household.She provides the reader with some important insights.

When she brings the young couple their midnight feast she introduces their characters to the reader. She reveals that Bertrande is beautiful with lucky two-coloured eyes. She says Martin is ugly but will become distinguished, and has the potential for greatness. She makes it clear that this marriage was made by the children's parents for their benefit and for the good of the whole community. '"And by and by you will appreciate all that your parents have done for you. And meanwhile what peace there is and what friendship in the village of Artigues!"' (p.10).

When Bertrande is grown and she agonises over her decision about pursuing Arnaud du Tilh, she turns to this trusted servant for advice. The housekeeper is again concerned for the welfare of the wider community. She notes how happy the household was in the time after Martin's apparent return. Bertrande's lawsuit has disturbed that contentment and the housekeeper suggests she withdraw her allegations. '"Madame, I would have you still be deceived. We were all happy then"' (p.75).

Q Do you know of any other texts that use the literary convention of the 'wise fool'?

Pierre Guerre

Pierre Guerre is Martin's uncle who comes to Artigues to serve as head of the household after M. Guerre's death and in the absence of the actual heir, Martin. He is a softer person than Martin's father had been but also, perhaps, a less effective farm manager. He and Bertrande work together to maintain the estate. Bertrande has an affection for him and he comes to believe and support her. He represents the solidity of the traditional way of life.

> She remembered then that he was not only her one supporter in the task which she had undertaken, but that he was also the one remaining defender of the old authority of her husband's house. He was that authority, simple and direct, without need of subterfuge or of superfluous charm, which before the coming of the stranger had kept them all in a secure and wholesome peace. He was for her that day a tradition more potent than the church. In her country the church had sometimes been denied, but even the Albigenses, hunted from town to town, from town to mountain cavern, and mercilessly destroyed for that denial, had never denied the tradition of which Pierre Guerre was the symbol (pp.77–8).

(The Albigenses were members of a vilified religious sect in existence between the eleventh and thirteenth centuries in southern France.)

The youngest sister

Martin's youngest sister is Bertrande's friend. She does not believe Bertrande's story, indeed she believes her mad, but she is kind and supportive of her sister-in-law. The girl is distressed by the upheaval that Bertrande's lawsuit brings upon the family and counsels her to abandon it.

> "Little sister," she answered in despair, "how can I deny the truth?"
>
> "It is only the truth for you, not for us," returned the weeping girl. "For the truth, that none of us believe, you would destroy us all. We shall never be happy again. The farm will never prosper again" (p.73).

The youngest sister also has a function in the text's discussion of the elusiveness of truth. She tries to make Bertrande understand that, for the family, this man is their brother and protector. For the time being he performs that role to their satisfaction.

Monsieur Guerre

Key quotes

'He sat ... vigilantly surveying his household, like some Homeric king, some ruler of an island commonwealth who could both plough and fight' (pp.16–17).

'Because of him the farm was safe, and therefore Artigues, and therefore Languedoc, and therefore France, and therefore the whole world was safe and as it should be' (p.17).

'"Madame, that my son should have become a thief is the greatest shame I have ever been asked to bear. Since he is my son, my only son, and since the welfare of the house depends upon the succession of an heir, I consider it my duty to forgive him. When he returns and confesses his crime, and has borne his punishment, I shall withdraw my anger. Until that time, no matter how distant it may be, rest assured, Madame, my anger shall exist"' (p.25).

Monsieur Guerre is a more powerful figure of authority than Pierre Guerre because he inhabits the position of *cap d'hostal* without gentleness. He acts in everything to secure the welfare of the family. He is an uncompromising father who insists upon obedience because he believes it necessary for the security of the system and the family. M. Guerre takes both the responsibility and authority of being head of the household very seriously.

Key point

Emphasis is placed in the text on Monsieur Guerre's responsibility as much as his authority. He is on several occasions referred to as just (p.16, p.19, p.25). While he can be a harsh man, his severity is placed in the context of his weighty responsibilities.

Toward Bertrande, Martin's father is kind if not affectionate. He is good to her in his way. When she produces an heir the family offers her more respect and privileges. Having Sanxi as an heir to survive him is important to M. Guerre, particularly after the disappearance of his own son, for his solitary purpose is the welfare and continuity of the family dynasty.

Q What advantages does living under the authority of M. Guerre bring to members of his household? What might be some of the disadvantages?

Madame Guerre

Bertrande's own parents feature little in the story. Martin's mother is a kind but distant figure. She upholds and enforces the traditional system. She guides the young wife over the estate that will one day be entrusted to the younger woman, and teaches Bertrande the duties of a wife, as she too must once have been taught. When Martin is punished for going on the bear hunt, she supports his father and tries to justify the beating (p.19). She supports the idea that only strict discipline will secure the family's survival.

Priest

The local parish priest holds a position of considerable power. He has responsibility for the spiritual welfare of the community. He is the church's representative in the village.

Key point

It is ironic that while Bertrande is motivated in her lawsuit by the fear of God, the priest counsels her to give up her suit against the impostor.

Q What is the priest's motivation in advising Bertrande to give up her action?

Arnaud du Tilh befriends the priest. They both have a level of learning and a concern for the community. The priest believes that Bertrande's lawsuit threatens the community's happiness. He is also concerned that she risks being responsible for the execution of an innocent man. He believes du Tilh's claim to be Martin Guerre and he values his company. Arnaud du Tilh has made sure that the priest favours him and discredits Bertrande's story. Du Tilh has manipulated the priest to side with him. The priest is unconcerned by the possibility of Bertrande's adultery because he is convinced that this man is Martin.

The priest recognises that this man is different to the '"raw, impatient youth ... thoughtless boy, selfish in the extreme"' who left years ago (p.71). Rather than doubting the man's identity, he attributes these changes to maturity. '"He had in him, it is true, the qualities of a great man. I like to think he has grown into that man"' (p.71). With the rest of the village, the priest seems to wilfully resist the idea that this man is an impostor.

THEMES & ISSUES

Perception and reality

Key quotes

'Even the room in which she slept in her aunt's house seemed turned around, and the sun rose in the west and shone through western windows all the morning' (p.33).

'... as he advanced from the shadow he seemed to Bertrande a stranger ... a man who might have been Martin's ancestor but not young Martin Guerre' (p.35).

'"... the picture seems to move, like people changing places in a dance"' (p.61).

The Wife of Martin Guerre explores the idea that reality is not fixed but changes according to the perception of the viewer. The narrative, in which one man successfully impersonates another, is a clear demonstration of competing realities, and the struggle of one individual to have her reality acknowledged.

The trial itself is documented by one of the judges whose perspective is both masculine and impersonal. Placing Bertrande's experience, thoughts and emotions at the centre of the story introduces a whole other set of concerns, and draws attention to the significance of perspective.

The text uses shifting perspectives to unsettle the notion of a single, universal and unchanging reality.

- When young Bertrande moves into her husband's home she notices how differently her father-in-law appears in the firelight than he had seemed in the torchlight of her wedding party (p.16).
- After the disappearance of her husband Bertrande has visions of Martin that fade and disappear. She believes she sees Martin in the forest, but it is not him and close up the stranger does not even resemble him (p.30).

- She imagines she can feel Martin's presence but the feeling fades and she is alone (p.30).
- She travels to Rieux to look for Martin and she stays with her aunt. In her aunt's house she becomes disoriented and thinks that the 'sun rose in the west and shone through western windows all the morning' (p.33).

These examples alert the reader to the occasions in the text that show how a character's perspective of events or people influences their idea of reality, and of the truth. Issues that arise here include the ways in which the various characters construct reality; how they justify their own beliefs; the persecution of Bertrande (and the construction of her as insane) for pursuing the truth about Arnaud du Tilh; and the authority of the powerful to construct the truth. These ideas will be explored later in this section.

In *The Wife of Martin Guerre* reality is filtered through different characters' perceptions of events. Reality is affected by different points of view and different circumstances. So, for example, Bertrande's sisters-in-law are utterly convinced that Arnaud is Martin. Bertrande is equally convinced that Arnaud is an impostor. They are each so sure of their own viewpoints that they are willing to swear to it in court.

The nature of deception

The Wife of Martin Guerre is the story of an extraordinary deception. Deception is an act of trickery, fraud or misrepresentation of the truth. Honesty and openness are qualities usually regarded as worthy within most value systems; religious and legal systems particularly encourage truthfulness. Consider, in contrast, the notion of the white lie: a harmless or trivial untruth. It is a deception that protects someone from information that might hurt them. Let's consider how these ideas are explored in the text.

When Arnaud du Tilh arrives to impersonate Martin, the family's memories of the real Martin have faded. Indeed, they are anxious for this man to be Martin. Bertrande will say to the real Martin, when he finally reappears at the trial, that her sin was occasioned by her great desire for his presence (p.90). Bertrande's suspicions are easily calmed by du Tilh's charm and cunning, that is, until they become so strong that they destroy the comfort that his presence brings.

His sisters firmly believe that the man who has returned to them is Martin, partly because it benefits their own situation. Nothing happens for them to want to challenge their certainty that he is their brother. The housekeeper and the priest both appear uncertain about the identity of Bertrande's husband; indeed their comments acknowledge a suspicion that he is not Martin Guerre. Yet in their desire to maintain the wellbeing of the community and their own comfort, they choose to support the impostor's claim. They are happy to remain deceived.

Q Why does her family continue to believe the impostor is Martin after Bertrande's accusations?

Her advisors all encourage Bertrande to undertake a deception of her own to secure the happiness of all concerned. They would have her pretend that Arnaud is her husband to maintain the happiness he has brought to them all.

Q What does this suggest about deception?

The major act of deception within the text – that is, Arnaud's impersonation of Martin – is not the only occasion of trickery. Martin tells Bertrande that he will only be absent for a week or so, but is gone for eight years and does not come home voluntarily, it seems, but only to defend his honour in court. Arnaud adds to his abuse of Bertrande when he tries to maintain the deception once her suspicions are aroused. He does this by using his influence and status to convince those around her that she is mad, so as to discredit her accusations.

As the person deceived, Bertrande is placed in a state of conflict, confusion and self-doubt. In fact, Arnaud's deception threatens Bertrande's mental stability. Arnaud further undermines Bertrande through his descriptions of her as insane. Her sense of disorientation and physical unwellness only heightens her fear of this, and she begins to believe his lies.

Arnaud's deception of Bertrande is also made possible because of the subservient role of the wife within this society, and the unquestioning obedience expected by Bertrande towards the man who is supposedly her husband. This value system makes it more difficult to question the identity of the imposter, because of the role he assumes as head of the household.

Q How was it possible for Bertrande to be deceived into mistaking Arnaud du Tilh for her husband?

Bertrande is disadvantaged by Martin's abandonment and compromised by Arnaud's deception. She chooses the truth over further deception. Yet the text shows that she sacrifices her place in the family, the happiness she finds with Arnaud, the legitimacy of her child, her faith in her religion and her confidence in the legal system to expose the deception. It suggests that her commitment to the truth is misguided, and that, perhaps, the continued deception would have been the most positive outcome.

Q Do you think the novella suggests that deception might at times be justified?

Q Are those who believe Arnaud's deception wilfully blind, or are they actually completely innocent of his deceit?

Social institutions and the individual

The Wife of Martin Guerre explores the ways in which the social institutions – the church and the legal system – that governed everyday life in sixteenth-century France regulated the lives of ordinary people. These social institutions established social order through laws, customs and other practices. For example, Bertrande's daily activities, as well as the more fundamental decisions she must make about her life, are influenced by the rules and conventions of the church, family, marriage and the law.

Let us look at each of the institutions that affect Bertrande and how the reader is positioned to view their role in Bertrande's life.

Religion

Key quote

'"I have sinned, through him, and you will not understand it even long enough to give me absolution!"' (p.72).

Bertrande is a devout Catholic. As such, she has developed a very strong sense of right and wrong. She strives to live by the church's morality and teachings. The fear of being involved in an adulterous relationship – of living in sin – leads to Bertrande becoming a 'tortured soul', as the guilt she feels weighs enormously on her conscience. The reader sees Bertrande undermined by guilt and the fear of sinning before God.

Bertrande relies on her religious faith, and the priest as representative of God, as her guides. In a state of conflict, she seeks the priest's confidence, wanting to confess the sins she believes she has committed, thereby seeking forgiveness. The priest does not provide this; indeed, he encourages her to stay with the false Martin, in spite of the possibility that he is not her husband.

The priest's friendship with Arnaud leads him to give Bertrande advice that is not consistent with church teaching, which is acceptable if he is indeed convinced of Arnaud's deception. However, it is possible that the priest is not convinced by Arnaud's deception, in which case he would be judging the situation from a more humane and pragmatic understanding of the situation rather than from the moral teachings of the church.

The narrative shows a very great gap between the ideals of religion and the practice of the clergy. Bertrande stays true to a strict application of the moral teachings of the church and, ultimately, appears to suffer as a result. The priest's actions, and his willingness to continue the deception (assuming he is wilfully blind to Arnaud's actions) for the benefits it brings, offers a more compassionate application of church law, and a more positive result for everyone.

Q What is the priest's motivation in encouraging Bertrande to go against the rules of her religion by staying with a man she believes is not her husband?

Q Is the novella critical of the church and the church's teaching?

Marriage

Key quotes

'Bertrande had not spoken to Martin in all her life until that morning, although she had often seen him; indeed she had not known until the evening before that a marriage had been arranged' (pp.5–6).

'Advantages there were, certainly, from the marriage, but for the present they were all for the two families of Guerre and de Rols' (p.11).

'… when he returned, if he should return after the death of his father, his authority would be as great as his father's then was, and to murmur against his treatment of her would then be improper in the highest degree' (p.27).

Marriage is called an institution because it is a code with regulations and conventions. The state and church sanction and recognise the union of men and women in marriage. Social and family expectations and practices also define marriage. The institution of marriage, altered by the context of time and place, determines the circumstances of individual marriages.

The marriage of Bertrande and Martin is typical of the time and place. It is an arranged marriage; the children play no part in the decision to be wed. Their lives together are mapped out; her marriage means Bertrande becomes part of Martin's family and must obey the rule of his father. She inherits specific responsibilities within the household – she must honour Martin, produce an heir, and attend to those under her care before her personal comfort or happiness. Bertrande is faithful to this code.

The narrative shows that Martin struggles to be content with his role on the farm and in the family, and that he feels restricted by the obligations upon him. When he leaves Bertrande, Martin breaks the arrangement between them. By contrast, Bertrande is attentive to her duty to the family and maintains her obedience to Martin in spite of the difficulties she faces because of his abandonment. Bertrande is unable to withdraw from her obligations to her (husband's) family; as a woman there were few (respectable) opportunities for independence in the sixteenth century.

Q How does the text suggest that Bertrande's distress is due to both Martin's rejection and to the institutions that restrict them both?

Q Why does Bertrande not have the same freedom as Martin to reject the institutions that govern her?

The author writes largely from the perspective of the abandoned wife, and the reader is positioned to condemn the family (apart from Martin's uncle) for their lack of support for Bertrande's cause.

Q Does the text suggest that Bertrande is disadvantaged by her loyalty to the family into which she has married?

The role of the family

The family plays several roles throughout the text. The family provides a relatively secure and stable existence for Bertrande, and gives her a certain status and respect. Despite her husband's abandonment of her, she remains a part of the family and is provided for. However, there is no tolerance for any lapses of loyalty to the family code by Bertrande. The reader, unlike the family, is privy to, and therefore sympathetic towards, Bertrande's thoughts and emotions. The family, on the other hand, does not consider the feelings of Bertrande as an individual, nor does she expect that they should.

Q Does Bertrande have any other choice but to remain within the family structure, whatever the consequences? Are there any alternatives for a woman in her position?

The novella suggests that even in arranged marriages, love, or great attachment, may grow between the couple. In her experiences with Martin and Arnaud, Bertrande becomes very emotionally attached and, in both cases, she loses the men at this point. Ultimately, though, marriage is presented to the reader as a form of entrapment for Bertrande. In the end, Martin's treatment of Bertrande shows her to be little more than her husband's property, to be dealt with as he sees fit.

The legal system

Key quotes

'Gradually a body of information was built up, minute details contributed now by one witness, now by another' (p.84).

'Of the thirty new witnesses, twelve declared themselves unable to make any decision regarding the identity of the accused. He might be either Martin Guerre or Arnaud du Tilh, for all they could observe. On the other hand, seven of the new witnesses were quite sure that he was du Tilh, and ten were equally convinced that he was Martin Guerre' (p.84).

The novella investigates the nature of the law: the way it works, its assumptions, its priorities, and its processes.

The legal process is structured around competing realities. Witnesses (in this case over one hundred) present wildly varying opinions. The legal system assumes that people have different views of the same events, but it attempts to determine the most probable version of reality based on the strength of evidence. That reality is then recognised by the court and this takes on the status of truth.

The law functions in the text, as in life, as a force for social control. People must obey the law to assure safety and security. In turn, the law protects the interests of society's members by guaranteeing them the opportunity to have any wrongs committed against them set right. Arnaud du Tilh, who is said to respect no law, is ultimately charged with acts that are seen as threatening the fabric of society. The judges punish him for betraying the laws of the institutions that regulate everyday life.

In the sixteenth century, the power of the law is determined by a complex process. The law claims its power in part by speaking in the name of the king who, in medieval belief, was thought to rule by divine right (because God had put him there as his earthly representative). Accordingly, the judges claim to be administering the law in the name of the king and God. In this way the authority of God was seen to be present in the law and gave it power. This underlies Bertrande's view of the law.

Bertrande respects the authority of the law and believes that it will deliver the truth. The author suggests, however, that Bertrande's faith might be mistaken and that Bertrande is alienated by the legal process that she hopes will restore her life to her. She expects that the law will acknowledge her version of truth and that this will make matters right. As the above discussion suggests, the law serves society, not only the individual. The law regards the wrong done to her as a wrong done to society as well. In this case, the punishment that is given to du Tilh, and the position that Bertrande is left in as a consequence, does not work in her favour.

Key point

Lewis draws attention to the ways in which the church, the family and the legal system regulate the lives of the characters. She demonstrates the extent to which the people with authority in these systems fail themselves to live up to their ideals. The text ultimately describes the failure of these institutions to provide their supposed goals of security, justice, and fairness.

Women and power

The text critically examines the status and position of women within society and social institutions. The author shows that women are prevented from being involved in decision-making processes and are therefore denied any real power over their own lives. They are unable to make choices about their lives and are limited to certain roles in family life. They have no alternative but to undertake the roles assigned to them.

Q Explore the role of each woman in the text and consider to what extent each is involved in making decisions about their own lives.

Q Discuss the impact of their lack of autonomy and power on their lives.

Individual roles and responsibilities

In the world of *The Wife of Martin Guerre*, people's roles in the family and in the community are well-defined. Each member of the family has tasks to perform that contribute to the running of the farm and household. Each person is important to the security and wellbeing of the community. In turn everyone has a position and identity determined by their place in the family.

As described in the background section of this guide, the feudal system depends upon a strictly defined and hierarchical order, that is, a system in which people are ranked according to social status, with the most senior having the most power. Relationships within this order are regulated by custom. Gender roles are firmly defined; men are involved in the physical labour of farming and women with the care of the family, children, household and domestic animals, such as poultry and pigs.

Marriages, such as the arranged marriage of Bertrande and Martin, were part of the social organisation of the feudal system. In the novella, Bertrande accepts her marriage and her role in the Guerre family without question. Her mother-in-law introduces her to the household and to her duties, as her own mother-in-law must have done (pp.14–15). Bertrande's status in the family is raised with the birth of her son, as she fulfils her responsibility to provide an heir for Martin.

The system was supposed to guarantee the protection of its members, but the family does not support Bertrande unconditionally. When she decides to take du Tilh to court they oppose her vigorously. Bertrande must justify her decisions at every turn.

Q Does the family fulfil its responsibilities to Bertrande, just as she tries to fulfil her responsibilities in return?

Bertrande's position in the household is disturbed when Arnaud uses his authority and position to convince the community that she is mad, so as to discredit her story. He manages to convince many people that Bertrande is unstable, and their collective hostility contributes to her feeling unwell. Her place in the family and community is unsettled by Arnaud's assertion that she is mad and by her continued rejection of him. This exercise of power assists Arnaud because it undermines Bertrande's role in the family.

The novella shows that Bertrande desires to maintain her place in the world and so follows the rules and customs of the institutions that order her life. She carries out the roles and responsibilities she is expected to fulfil. She acts faithfully within these systems even when challenged by figures of authority, such as the priest and Arnaud, and when pressured to compromise her ideals. Despite behaving with integrity, she is abused by representatives of the institutions she seeks to honour. She loses the security and identity that she depends upon.

Q Bertrande's role as dutiful wife fails to protect her from misrepresentation and unjust judgements. Discuss.

Justice

The novella explores issues of justice of various kinds. Justice is a difficult concept to define, and the reader sees that the assessment of an outcome as just or unjust depends on the participant's viewpoint. The text makes a distinction between justice and truth. It also makes a distinction between the court's ability to administer legal and moral justice.

The reader is positioned to regard the return of Martin Guerre and his treatment of Bertrande as very unjust. From Bertrande's perspective, however, justice is done with the public recognition of Arnaud's deception. Bertrande would consider Martin's subsequent treatment of her as just, according to the values of the time.

Legal justice

The final result – the conviction and execution of Arnaud du Tilh – is not satisfying for Bertrande. The tension between her legal victory and her personal distress reveals the inability of the legal process to administer justice, as well as the law's inability to appreciate Bertrande's situation. The text suggests the law was (and is) limited by the perspectives of those who apply it.

Bertrande has high expectations that the court will confirm her view that the man claiming to be her husband is an impostor. She is distressed when, at the end of the trial at Rieux, the judges sentence du Tilh to death. She does not desire the death of the man for whom she once had a great affection, she only desires the truth to be publicly acknowledged. (This alarm is later used against her, ironically, as evidence that the accused is her husband.)

The court is guided by its responsibility to apply the law for the good of the whole community and not only for individual satisfaction. Bertrande is distanced from the process of the trial she brings about because she and the court are seeking different outcomes. Consequently, she is not served by the final decision. Her 'solitary justice' comes at the expense of her security and place in the family, her personal contentment and her relationships. The author suggests that, despite the success of her lawsuit, justice is not achieved.

Q Arnaud du Tilh is convicted of multiple crimes but Martin Guerre is convicted of none. Is this just?

Moral justice

The author positions the reader to consider the ideal of justice as distinct from legal justice – the administration of law by the courts. Moral justice takes into account something beyond the mere appreciation of legal rules; it questions whether a decision can be legally correct but also unfair.

Bertrande acts according to her principles. Once she recognises that Arnaud is not her husband she must reject him, in spite of her affection for him. Bertrande pursues her case in the face of opposition from almost every person in her life. She receives only self-interested pleas from others that she accept du Tilh as her husband. By contrast, Bertrande is motivated by her duty to her marriage, family and religion. She behaves with integrity within these frameworks but is never given support to do so. There is no recognition of the communal ideals and interests that motivate her pursuit of the truth.

The legal decision that supports Bertrande's claim that du Tilh is not her husband also implicitly supports Martin, who abandoned her, and his cruel accusation that she was *wilfully* deceived and is herself responsible for the dishonour brought upon him. No consideration is made by the court for the difficulties under which she laboured after she had been abandoned by her husband. No consideration is able to be made for the affection with which she held Arnaud and the good he does for her and for her family.

The narrative gives Bertrande's perspective in sympathetic detail so the reader feels the injustice of her situation, in spite of the ultimate decision of the courts in her favour. The reader is guided by the narrative to sympathise with her and to be critical of the failures of the court to produce just outcomes.

Q Do you think Bertrande's situation suggests that moral justice is not achieved?

What is truth?

Key quotes

'I am destroying the happiness of my family. And why? For the sake of a truth, to free myself from a deceit which was consuming and killing me' (p.81).

'"What would you have, my sister? The truth is only the truth. I cannot change it"' (p.81).

'"It is true only for you"' (p.81).

In *The Wife of Martin Guerre,* the notion of a fixed and definite truth is challenged by the deceit of Arnaud du Tilh. The truth about Bertrande's situation is revealed with the appearance of the real Martin Guerre. Martin's arrival in the courtroom at Toulouse establishes the truth that Martin is alive and that Arnaud du Tilh has been impersonating him. This truth is *only then* no longer a matter for doubt or question. It is *the* truth because it is verified by his physical presence.

At another level, the novella questions the notion that truth is absolute and universal. Martin's presence opposite Arnaud du Tilh highlights the ways in which the 'reality' of the false Martin Guerre is constructed. There are numerous witnesses in the courtroom who remain convinced that his (and their) truth is correct, only to have it exposed as false with the appearance of the real Martin Guerre. The text shows how individual perspectives can determine reality without reference to the external and verifiable reality. It also suggests that the legal system cannot always reveal the truth.

The novella makes observations about important concepts, such as reality, truth, justice and the law, that are as relevant today as they were in the sixteenth century. The text is critical of the institutions that govern people's lives and define their world, and their inability to accommodate certain individuals and groups in society.

Q Discuss the different 'sources of truth' explored in this novella. Examples include physical, observable facts as truth, interpretation of evidence, beliefs of the church and the authority of God, and the processes of the legal system.

QUESTIONS & ANSWERS

This section focuses on your own analytical writing on the text, and gives you strategies for producing high-quality responses in your coursework and exam essays.

Essay topics

1 "Madame Guerre opened certain chests filled with bran and showed the young girl the coats of mail of the ancestors, thus preserved from rust. She did all this, as Bertrande well knew, that the young wife might understand the household which she would one day be called upon to direct."
What is Bertrande's status in the Guerre household? Consider her role before and after the deaths of Martin's parents.

2 'Bertrande is a courageous woman who does not deserve her fate.' Discuss.

3 "It is no more than just to remember that he has been kind to us – kind to all, save me, and kind even to me after a strange fashion."
'It would have been better for everyone in the Guerre household if Bertrande had accepted Arnaud du Tilh as her husband.' Discuss.

4 'Bertrande is selfish in her pursuit of legal justice.' To what extent do you agree?

5 'Bertrande's dedication to the truth, described as "bitter, solitary justice", reveals her to be naive and idealistic.' Discuss.

6 Do you think Arnaud du Tilh was an honourable man who suffered an unjust fate?

7 'The marriage of Bertrande and Martin brings all sorts of advantages to their community but none to the couple.' Discuss.

8 'The feudal system empowers men and the community. Women, however, are left powerless.' How is this shown in *The Wife of Martin Guerre*?

9 "Even the room in which she slept in her aunt's house seemed turned around, and the sun rose in the west and shone through western windows all the morning."
'*The Wife of Martin Guerre* shows that "reality" depends on individual perception.' Discuss.

10 'Arnaud du Tilh is found guilty of being an impostor at Rieux and not guilty at Toulouse. This suggests that the legal process is about legal justice rather than truth.' Discuss.

11 'Bertrande is initially the only person who believes that du Tilh is an impostor. Her family and the priest are motivated by self-interest when they encourage her to abandon her legal suit.' Do you agree?

12 "You, and you only, Madame, are answerable for the dishonour which has befallen me."
To what extent is Bertrande to blame for the situation confronting the Guerre family?

Analysing a sample topic

'Arnaud du Tilh is found guilty of being an impostor at Rieux and not guilty at Toulouse. This suggests that the legal process is about legal justice rather than truth.' Discuss.

This essay topic takes a characteristic form: first, a contention about what the text 'shows' (or 'suggests'), then a stem word or phrase, usually 'discuss' or 'do you agree?' To consider this topic, you need to explain how the text balances truth with legal justice. The theme is worked out in the text with respect to Bertrande's sense that she is seeking to have the truth acknowledged in the courts. This means that you must focus on the contrast between Bertrande's aim and the court processes. By doing this you will demonstrate knowledge of the text. For instance:

> In *The Wife of Martin Guerre* Bertrande justifies her pursuit of the unreal Martin Guerre by saying, 'The truth is only the truth. I cannot change it'. Her sister-in-law claims that it is 'the truth only for you'. Bertrande resorts to the law to

> establish what she believes is the truth. The legal process in the text shows, however, that the truth is only just stumbled upon. The reappearance of Martin Guerre forces the judges to change their verdict at the last minute. The novella reveals that the courts rely on the testimony of witnesses and other evidence to prove the case before them. Their realm is not truth but legal justice. They administer the law.

It is necessary to define the terms 'truth' and 'justice'. The paragraphs might then be organised around the understandings of Bertrande and the judges of their tasks.

- Bertrande is motivated to pursue the man she claims is an impostor all the way to the courts for the sake of truth.
- She hopes to be rid of Arnaud du Tilh (pp.51–2, p.66). She does not want him to be punished and certainly not executed (p.69).
- Bertrande is convinced that the truth is definite and attainable (p.73, p.81). Minor incidents in the text suggest that reality is a matter of perception (pp.30–1, p.33).
- The priest and her family dispute Bertrande's reality (pp.71–3). Arnaud du Tilh attempts to convince everyone that Bertrande is mad to discredit her story (p.57).
- Bertrande is pushed to take legal action to secure her freedom from the imposition of du Tilh (p.61, p.64).
- The courts take control of Bertrande's cause because they understand the accusations against du Tilh as a transgression against society (p.92).
- The trials are structured around the gathering of evidence and of testimonies of witnesses (pp.6–9, pp.84–7). The imperfection of the trial process is emphasised in the novella. The court can only weigh the evidence and look for proof.
- Bertrande is distanced from the process, which becomes something much different from her personal quest for truth and freedom (p.69).

- Consider the relevance of a discussion about truth and justice in contemporary society.

In conclusion make sure you draw out the general issues and connect them with how this plays out in the text. For example, consider the way the novella shows that Bertrande is not assisted by the justice system. As a medieval woman she is oppressed by the values and institutions of her society.

Another approach to the topic: disagreement with the contention

A different approach is required if you choose to disagree with the contention. Make it clear that you disagree with the statement by using words such as 'while' and 'although'. For example:

> While the courts in Rieux and Toulouse differ in their conclusions about the prisoner in ways that unsettle the notion that truth and justice can accord, the truth is ultimately revealed. Although Bertrande must pursue her case through the court system, her case is finally proven by the appearance of Martin Guerre in the courtroom. This suggests that, while a flawed system, the legal process is able to achieve a just and true outcome.

This is a more difficult approach but one might argue that justice and truth are both changeable concepts and that the legal system accounts for this.

- Bertrande stays focused on having the real truth of du Tilh's identity acknowledged and legitimised by the courts.
- For all the text's discussion of the unreliability of the legal system, Bertrande is freed of both her husbands and leaves the courtroom in Toulouse in quiet triumph.
- Martin's reappearance proves the notion of absolute truth.

In conclusion, use evidence from the text to justify faith in the ability of the judicial system to locate the truth and administer justice.

SAMPLE ANSWER

"You, and you only, Madame, are answerable for the dishonour which has befallen me."

To what extent is Bertrande to blame for the situation confronting the Guerre family?

The feudal system under which the Guerre family lives and prospers demands that the *cap d'hostal* be paid obedience. As Madame Guerre says to her son after his father punishes him severely for acting independently, 'If you have no obedience for your father, your son will have none for you, and then what will become of the family? Ruin.' Under this hierarchical and patriarchal system, the family honour rests on the behaviour of all who come under its jurisdiction, including sons, wives and servants. Therefore, it is clear that although Bertrande betrays her husband, Martin Guerre himself is also to blame for the family's shame, since he abandons his responsibilities. Likewise, Arnaud behaves in a manner that violates the requirements of society, as well as of the church, at the time and leads Bertande into 'sin'. Other members of the Guerre household, including the housekeeper and Martin's sisters, willingly accept the impostor as their master and brother. Finally, the feudal system itself can also be blamed for the situation confronting the Guerre family, who are led to accept Arnaud du Tilh as Martin Guerre in order to preserve the order and harmony of the household and estate.

Bertrande may be technically guilty of betraying her husband, but many other individuals must share the blame, the first amongst them being her husband. Martin is disobedient to his father; he steals, and deserts his home and inheritance. Most importantly, Martin abandons his young wife and their child 'in the height of her great passion'. In the afterword, Pasquier, commenting on the real case, judges Martin 'for having been by his absence the cause of this wrongdoing'.

It is also Martin's own personality that is to blame for Bertrande's initial acceptance of Arnaud. Where Martin was reserved, Arnaud is warm and kind. It is this difference that at first seduces her but later alerts her to his real identity: 'I see the flesh and bone of Martin Guerre, but in them I see dwelling the spirit of another man.'

Of course, Arnaud du Tilh is also to blame for bringing shame upon the Guerre family and his own. His crimes of plagiat and imposture surely set Bertrande on her own course of deceit and disobedience. He goes as far as encouraging Bertrande and those around her to believe her mad, in order to discredit her doubts about his identity. His personal charm also makes him culpable for the situation faced by the Guerre household: 'The vigour of the man [is] contagious', and so Bertrande 'surrender[s] herself to his love'. When Arnaud arrives, 'the loneliness of the house dissipated' and the household, not just Bertrande, accepts him as their master.

Martin's own sisters believe Arnaud to be their brother and place pressure on Bertrande to agree. Her sister-in-law rejects Bertrande's suggestion that Arnaud is an impostor, telling her, 'it is the truth only for you'. The pressure placed on Bertrande to suppress her doubts by those around her make Martin's sisters, Uncle Pierre and the priest, all of whom have more authority than she does, equally culpable in perpetuating the deceit. The 'estate prospered' following the return of the master and protector and no-one wants to see him as otherwise.

This response is in large part a result of a patriarchal system and one in which the rule of law is valued above sentiment. Bertrande may be guilty of hoping that the kinder man is her husband, but the social and religious systems that constrain her choices and the choices of those around her are also fundamentally at fault for the difficult situation faced by the Guerre household.

As a woman of her time, Bertrande's religious beliefs make her feel enormous guilt at sleeping with a man she knows is not her husband. On his return, Martin accuses her of having known that Arnaud was an impostor, charging her with 'wilful blindness' on the basis that as his wife, she should have a more intimate knowledge of her husband than anyone else. Ironically, she has been pleading with the authorities to declare Arnaud an impostor, but her lowly status as a woman means that the court does not 'sufficiently credit [her] story and [her] grief'. Men are to decide her fate, despite Martin's own admission that her word should be enough. Consequently, Bertrande assumes the guilt of du Tilh's actions. However, it is clear that others are just as responsible. Moreover, Martin is a harsh and inflexible character, whose judgement of his wife is presented as unjust; indeed it is this very harshness that is testament to the fact that he is truly the real Martin Guerre.

Although Martin blames his wife and says that his uncle's and sisters' behaviour do not excuse her, Bertrande cannot be held solely responsible for the tragedy besetting the house of Guerre. This is a tragedy born out of feudal patriarchy, inflexible law and the protagonists' own natures.

REFERENCES & READING

Text

Lewis, Janet, *The Wife of Martin Guerre*, Penguin Books, Camberwell, 1977.

References

Chojnacka, Monica and Wiesner-Hanks, Merry E., *Ages of woman, Ages of man: sources in European social history, 1400–1750*, Longman, 2002.

Cuddon, J.A., *The Penguin Dictionary of Literary Terms and Literary Theory*, Penguin, Harmondsworth, 1992.

Davies, Norman, *Europe: A History*, Oxford University Press, Oxford, 1996.

Duby, Georges, *Love and marriage in the Middle Ages*, Polity Press, Cambridge, 1994.

McMurtry, Larry, 'The Return of Janet Lewis' *New York Review of Books*, 45:10 (1998 June 11), (www.nybooks.com/articles/ 822).

Zemon Davis, Natalie, *The Return of Martin Guerre*, Harvard University Press, Cambridge Mass., 1983.

Film

The Return of Martin Guerre dir. Daniel Vigne.

Websites

http://www.lepg.org/sixteen.htm

http://www.arts.adelaide.edu.au/personal/DHart/Films/ReturnMartinGuerre.html